MW01228044

CHATGPT F

The Ultimate Beg
Leveraging A

Christoph

Self Pub

INTRODUCTION

Welcome to "ChatGPT for Profit," a journey into the transformative world of artificial intelligence and its untapped potential to revolutionize your approach to business, marketing, and revenue generation. I'm Chris Dessi, and I'm thrilled to share with you the insights, strategies, and stories that have not only shaped my career but also the trajectory of companies I've had the privilege to lead and advise.

As we embark on this adventure together, I want you to feel both welcomed and excited. The realm of AI, particularly ChatGPT, offers a vast landscape of opportunities waiting to be explored. Whether you're an entrepreneur, a marketer, or simply curious about the future of technology, this book is your gateway to understanding how AI can not only enhance your business operations but also significantly contribute to your bottom line.

"ChatGPT for Profit" is more than just a book; it's a comprehensive guide designed to equip you with the knowledge and tools necessary to navigate the ever-evolving world of AI. Through real-world examples, practical advice, and actionable strategies, you'll discover how to leverage ChatGPT and other AI technologies to outpace competition, innovate product offerings, and create unparalleled customer experiences.

But I didn't want to stop there. To ensure you're not just passively consuming information but actively engaging with it, each chapter concludes with a quiz. These quizzes are crafted to reinforce key concepts, provoke thought, and stimulate your creative thinking about how to apply what you've learned to your unique circumstances.

Moreover, for those who seek to dive deeper, my blog at www.christopherdessi.com serves as an extension of this book. There, you'll find additional resources, ongoing discussions, and the latest insights into AI, digital marketing, and personal development. It's a space where learning continues, and ideas flourish.

So, as you turn these pages, I invite you to open your mind to the possibilities that AI presents. This is not just about the future of technology; it's about the future of your success. Let's explore together how ChatGPT can become an integral part of your profit-making strategy, transforming not just how you do business, but how you think about potential itself.

Welcome to "ChatGPT for Profit." Let's turn the page and begin.

ISBN: 9798320619880

Cover design by: Chris Dessi
Library of Congress Control Number: 2018675309
Printed in the United States of America

For Talia & Olivia. Daddy loves you.

CONTENTS

CHATGPT FOR PROFIT

The Ultimate Beginner's Guide To Leveraging Ai In Business

by
Chris Dessi

CHAPTER 1 DEFINING AI

Artificial Intelligence (AI) is a field of computer science that focuses on creating systems capable of performing tasks that typically require human intelligence. These tasks include learning, reasoning, problem-solving, perception, and understanding language. AI systems are designed to operate with varying levels of autonomy, ranging from simple automation to complex decision-making processes that mimic human thought.

History of AI

The concept of artificial intelligence has been a subject of fascination and study for centuries, but it wasn't until the mid-20th century that AI became a formal field of academic research. The term "Artificial Intelligence" was first coined by John McCarthy in 1956 during the Dartmouth Conference, where the discipline was born. Early AI research in the 1950s and 1960s focused on problem-solving and symbolic methods.

In the 1970s, the field of AI expanded to include knowledge-based systems and expert systems, which attempted to encode expert knowledge in specific domains.

The 1980s saw the rise of machine learning, where AI systems were developed to learn from data and improve over time. The advent of the internet and the exponential increase in data availability in the 1990s and 2000s provided a significant boost to AI research and applications. In recent years, advancements in computational power, data availability, and algorithmic innovation have led to significant breakthroughs in AI, particularly in deep learning, which has enabled AI to achieve remarkable feats in image and speech recognition, natural language processing, and autonomous systems.

Types of AI

AI can be categorized into different types based on its capabilities and functionalities. Narrow AI, also known as weak AI, refers to AI systems that are designed to perform a single task or a narrow range of tasks. These systems are quite common and include voice assistants, image recognition software, and recommendation engines. General AI, or strong AI, is a theoretical form of AI that would have the ability to understand, learn, and apply knowledge in a way that is indistinguishable from human intelligence. This type of AI does not yet exist. Another way to classify AI is based on its learning capabilities, such as supervised learning, unsupervised learning, and reinforcement learning, each with its own set of algorithms and applications.

* * *

AI in the Business Context

Role of AI in Business

In the business world, AI plays a crucial role in driving innovation, efficiency, and competitive advantage. AI technologies are used to automate routine tasks, analyze large volumes of data, and provide insights that inform strategic decisions. AI is also instrumental in enhancing customer experiences through personalization and improving operational efficiencies across various business functions such as marketing, sales, and supply chain management.

Benefits of AI in Business

The benefits of AI in business are manifold. AI can process and analyze data at a scale beyond human capability, leading to more informed decision-making. It can automate repetitive and time-consuming tasks, allowing employees to focus on higher-value work. AI also enables businesses to provide personalized experiences to customers, improve product quality, and optimize supply chains. Moreover, AI can help businesses identify new opportunities and revenue streams by uncovering patterns and insights that would otherwise remain hidden.

Challenges of AI in Business

Despite its benefits, AI also presents several challenges for businesses. Implementing AI requires significant investment in technology and talent, and there may be a steep learning curve associated with its adoption. Data privacy and security are major concerns, as AI systems often require access to sensitive information. Additionally, there is the risk of AI perpetuating biases if the data used to train AI systems are not representative or if the algorithms are not designed carefully. Finally, businesses must navigate the ethical implications of AI, ensuring that its use aligns with societal values and norms.

Utilizing AI to Increase Organizational Efficiency

In the digital era, the adaptation and integration of artificial intelligence (AI) into business processes have become not just advantageous but essential for staying ahead. As we delve into the practical applications and transformative potential of AI, it's imperative to recognize its pivotal role in enhancing organizational efficiency, driving innovation, and reshaping marketing strategies.

The Onset of AI's Mainstream Adoption

Reflecting on the evolution of social media and its eventual ubiquity, AI's trajectory appears remarkably similar. Just as social media transitioned from a niche to a dominant form of communication, AI is on the brink of becoming fundamental to how businesses operate and engage with their customers. This comparison underscores the importance of early adoption and adaptation to AI technologies to maintain a competitive edge.

From Skepticism to Strategic Integration

The journey of integrating AI within Diamond Standard showcases the transformative power of AI in marketing and operational strategies. Diamond Standard, the world's first regulator-approved diamond commodity, leveraged AI to scale its marketing efforts, improve customer engagement, and enhance operational efficiencies. This strategic pivot was not without its challenges, requiring a comprehensive understanding of AI's capabilities and limitations.

AI as a Catalyst for Marketing Innovation

The utilization of AI in marketing at Diamond Standard is a testament to its potential to revolutionize traditional marketing paradigms. Through targeted and personalized communication, advanced analytics, and automated workflows, AI enabled Diamond Standard to engage effectively with its audience, ensuring the right message reached the right people at the right time.

Tech Stack Transformation and AI Integration

The transition from conventional software solutions to a unified AI-powered tech stack, including Zoho's suite of applications, marked a significant milestone in Diamond Standard's journey. This integration facilitated seamless operations, from sales and marketing to customer service, illustrating AI's role in creating efficient, scalable business processes.

Content Strategy Reimagined

AI's impact on content strategy and search engine optimization (SEO) was profound. Utilizing tools like ChatGPT, Diamond Standard crafted content that resonated with its target audience, significantly increasing organic traffic and engagement. This strategic content creation, underpinned by AI analysis and optimization, positioned Diamond Standard as a thought leader in the diamond investment space.

The Future of AI in Business

Looking ahead, the potential of AI to drive business growth and innovation is limitless. However, it's crucial to approach AI integration with a strategic mindset, focusing on areas where it can add the most value and enhance human efforts rather than replace them. The success story of Diamond Standard serves as a blueprint for leveraging AI to achieve operational excellence and competitive differentiation.

AI is not just a technological advancement; it's a strategic asset that can transform every aspect of a business. By embracing AI, organizations can unlock new opportunities for growth, innovation, and efficiency.

Quick Facts & Statistics

AI in Business: By the Numbers

Challenges & Concerns

AI and Business Strategy

Incorporating AI into Business Strategy

To leverage AI effectively, businesses must integrate it into their overall strategy. This involves identifying key areas where AI can add value, setting clear objectives for AI initiatives, and ensuring alignment with the company's broader goals. It also requires building the necessary infrastructure, such as data storage and processing capabilities, and fostering a culture that embraces innovation and change.

Business owners of all sizes can leverage ChatGPT to expedite monotonous tasks. Here are some creative ways you can leverage ChatGPT notmatter what your role.

Content Creation: Users frequently request help in generating ideas for blog posts, social media content, email marketing campaigns, and website copy that are engaging and tailored to their target audience.

Brand Messaging: Crafting compelling brand messages, value propositions, and mission statements that resonate with the audience and differentiate the brand from competitors.

Product Descriptions: Writing detailed and persuasive product descriptions for e-commerce sites, highlighting features and benefits to encourage purchases.

SEO Optimization: Assistance in optimizing content with keywords, meta descriptions, and titles to improve search engine rankings and visibility.

Social Media Strategy: Developing strategies for social media marketing, including post ideas, scheduling, and engagement tactics to build a following and promote brand awareness.

Email Campaigns: Creating email marketing campaigns, including promotional emails, newsletters, and automated sequences to engage subscribers and drive conversions.

Advertising Copy: Writing copy for online ads, such as Google AdWords or Facebook ads, that captures attention and compels the target audience to take action.

Market Research: Formulating prompts to conduct market research, including survey questions and interview scripts to gather insights about customer preferences and behaviors.

Competitive Analysis: Requests for assistance in analyzing competitors' marketing strategies, identifying opportunities for differentiation, and benchmarking performance.

Marketing Plan Development: Help in outlining comprehensive marketing plans, including objectives, target markets, channels, budgets, and KPIs to guide marketing efforts.

These prompts cover a wide range of marketing activities and are indicative of the diverse needs of users looking to leverage AI for enhancing their marketing efforts. Each prompt can be tailored to fit the specific context and goals of the user's business or project.

Pro Tip: When writing a prompt - nomatter the topic, ask ChatGPT to "Act like a _____ expert" before you add your prompt.

For example: "Act like a marketing expert and create a marketing plan for a midsized manufacturer making bike parts."

AI and Competitive Advantage

AI can be a source of competitive advantage by enabling businesses to operate more efficiently, make better decisions, and offer unique products and services. Companies that adopt AI early and strategically are often able to outperform their competitors by improving customer satisfaction, reducing costs, and accelerating time to market for new offerings.

AI and Business Model Innovation

AI also has the potential to drive business model innovation. By leveraging AI, companies can create new value propositions, enhance customer engagement, and develop new revenue models. For example, AI can enable subscription-based services that offer personalized recommendations or predictive maintenance services that reduce downtime for customers.

AI and Business Operations

AI in Marketing

AI is transforming marketing by enabling more targeted and personalized campaigns. AI-powered tools can analyze consumer behavior, predict trends, and optimize marketing spend. This leads to more effective marketing strategies that resonate with consumers and drive engagement.

AI in Customer Service

In customer service, AI is used to enhance the customer experience through chatbots and virtual assistants that provide instant, 24/7 support. AI can also help businesses analyze customer feedback and improve service quality by identifying areas for improvement.

AI in Supply Chain Management

AI applications in supply chain management include demand forecasting, inventory optimization, and logistics planning. By analyzing data from various sources, AI can help businesses anticipate market changes, reduce waste, and improve the efficiency of their supply chains.

Further Reading

If you're interested in delving deeper into the fascinating world of AI in business, here are some recommended books and articles:

For online resources, consider these articles:

AI and Business Ethics

Ethical Considerations in AI

As AI becomes more prevalent in business, ethical considerations must be addressed. This includes ensuring that AI systems are transparent, fair, and do not infringe on individual privacy. Companies must also consider the societal impact of AI, such as potential job displacement and the need for re-skilling workers.

AI and Data Privacy

Data privacy is a critical issue in the age of AI. Businesses must navigate complex regulations and ensure that customer data is collected, stored, and used in compliance with legal and ethical standards. This includes obtaining consent for data use and protecting data from unauthorized access.

AI and Fairness

Ensuring that AI systems are fair and unbiased is a significant challenge. Businesses must be vigilant in monitoring for biases in AI decision-making and take steps to mitigate any discriminatory effects. This involves using diverse datasets for training AI and regularly auditing AI systems for fairness.

AI and the Future of Business

Emerging AI Technologies

The field of AI is rapidly evolving, with new technologies

emerging regularly. These include advancements in natural language processing, which is improving the ability of AI to understand and generate human language, and quantum computing, which has the potential to revolutionize AI by processing information at unprecedented speeds.

AI and Business Trends

AI is shaping future business trends, such as the rise of autonomous systems in transportation and logistics, the increasing use of AI in healthcare diagnostics, and the growth of AI-powered financial technology. Businesses must stay informed about these trends to capitalize on the opportunities they present.

AI and Future Workforce

The impact of AI on the workforce is a topic of much debate. While AI may automate certain jobs, it also creates new opportunities for employment in areas such as AI development, data analysis, and AI system maintenance. Businesses and educational institutions must work together to prepare the workforce for the AI-driven economy.

Review Questions

1. What is the definition of AI?
2. What is one of the benefits of AI in Business?
3. What is one of the challenges of AI in Business?
4. What is one way AI can be incorporated into Business Strategy?
5. What is one ethical consideration in AI?

UNDERSTANDING AI TECHNOLOGIES

CHAPTER 2 UNDERSTANDING AI TECHNNOLOGIES

Understanding AI Technologies

Definition of Machine Learning Machine Learning (ML) is a subset of artificial intelligence that focuses on the development of algorithms and statistical models that enable computers to perform tasks without explicit instructions. Instead, these systems learn and make decisions based on patterns and inferences from data. The core idea is to allow machines to learn automatically without human intervention or assistance and adjust actions accordingly.

Types of Machine Learning

There are three primary types of machine learning: supervised learning, unsupervised learning, and reinforcement learning. Supervised learning involves training a moAI Teel on a labeled dataset, which means that each training example is paired with an output label. Unsupervised learning, on the other hand, deals with unlabeled data, and the system tries to learn the patterns and structure from the input data. Reinforcement learning is a type of machine learning where an agent learns to make decisions by performing certain actions and observing the rewards or penalties that result from those actions.

Applications of Machine Learning

Machine learning has a wide array of applications across various industries. In finance, ML algorithms are used for fraud detection and credit scoring. In healthcare, they assist in diagnosing diseases and personalizing treatment plans. In retail, machine learning enhances customer service through personalized shopping experiences and inventory management. Additionally, ML is used in self-driving cars, recommendation systems like those on Netflix or Amazon, and in natural language processing applications such as voice-activated assistants.

Deep Learning

Definition of Deep Learning

Deep Learning is a subset of machine learning that uses neural networks with many layers (hence "deep") to analyze various factors with a structure similar to the human neural system. Deep learning models are capable of automatic feature extraction from raw data, which is a significant advantage over traditional machine learning models that require manual feature extraction.

Neural Networks

Neural networks are a series of algorithms that mimic the operations of a human brain to recognize relationships between vast amounts of data. They are composed of nodes, or "neurons," which are connected together and transmit signals to each other. These connections have weights that are adjusted during the training process, and the strength of the signal that a neuron sends through a connection is determined by the weight of that connection. Deep neural networks, which are an essential part of deep learning, consist of multiple layers of neurons, and they are capable of learning complex patterns thanks to their depth.

Applications of Deep Learning

Deep learning has revolutionized many fields such as computer vision and natural language processing. In computer vision, deep learning algorithms are used for image recognition, object detection, and facial recognition. In natural language processing, deep learning models are behind language translation services, chatbots, and voice recognition systems. Deep learning is also used in autonomous vehicles for real-time decision-making and in medical fields for analyzing medical images to detect and diagnose diseases.

Test Your Knowledge

Let's see how well you've understood the applications of deep learning. Try to answer the following questions:

Remember: Deep learning is a subset of machine learning that uses neural networks with many layers (hence 'deep') to analyze various levels of data, such as images or text. It's a key technology behind many advanced AI applications.

Natural Language Processing

Definition of Natural Language Processing

Natural Language Processing (NLP) is a field at the intersection of computer science, artificial intelligence, and linguistics. It involves the development of algorithms and systems that enable computers to understand, interpret, and generate human language. NLP aims to bridge the gap between human communication and computer understanding, allowing for seamless interaction.

Components of Natural Language Processing

NLP consists of several components that help in processing human language. These include syntax, which is the arrangement of words in a sentence to make grammatical sense; semantics, which is the meaning conveyed by a text; pragmatics, which deals with the use of language in social contexts and the ways in which people produce and comprehend meanings; discourse, which involves the structure of texts longer than one sentence; and speech, which includes the aspects of recognizing and generating spoken language.

Applications of Natural Language Processing

NLP applications are becoming increasingly common in everyday technology. Examples include spell check, autocomplete, spam filters, voice-activated GPS systems, and personal assistant applications like Siri and Alexa. In business, NLP is used for sentiment analysis to gauge consumer opinions, chatbots for customer service, and machine translation for global communication. NLP is also pivotal in healthcare for extracting information from clinical texts and in the legal field for document analysis.

Computer Vision

Definition of Computer Vision

Computer Vision is a field of artificial intelligence that trains computers to interpret and understand the visual world. Using digital images from cameras and videos and deep learning models, machines can accurately identify and classify objects —

and then react to what they "see."

Techniques in Computer Vision

Techniques in computer vision include image recognition and object detection, which are used to identify objects or features within an image. Another technique is segmentation, which partitions an image into multiple segments to simplify or change the representation of an image into something more meaningful and easier to analyze. Motion analysis and pattern detection are also important techniques that contribute to the understanding of the visual scenes.

Applications of Computer Vision

The applications of computer vision are vast and varied. In the automotive industry, computer vision is a key component of autonomous vehicle technology, enabling cars to make sense of their surroundings. In retail, computer vision is used for checkout-free shopping experiences, inventory tracking, and customer behavior analysis. Security and surveillance also rely heavily on computer vision for facial recognition and activity monitoring. In healthcare, computer vision assists in medical image analysis for diagnostics and treatment planning.

Further Reading

If you're interested in exploring more about the applications of computer vision in various industries, visit www.christopherdessi.com/resources

For online resources, consider these articles:

Robotics

Definition of Robotics

Robotics is an interdisciplinary branch of engineering and science that includes mechanical engineering, electronic engineering, information engineering, computer science, and others. Robotics deals with the design, construction, operation, and use of robots, as well as computer systems for their control, sensory feedback, and information processing.

Types of Robots

Robots can be classified into several different types based on their capabilities and applications. Industrial robots are used for manufacturing and can perform tasks such as welding, painting, and assembly. Service robots, on the other hand, perform tasks for humans such as cleaning, delivery, and personal assistance. There are also specialized robots designed for specific tasks like surgical robots in healthcare, exploration robots in space and underwater, and humanoid robots that mimic human actions and interactions.

Applications of Robotics

Robotics has applications in a wide range of industries. In manufacturing, robots automate repetitive tasks, increasing efficiency and safety. In healthcare, robots assist in surgeries, rehabilitation, and caring for the elderly. Robots are also used in hazardous environments like space exploration, deep-sea exploration, and disaster response, where they can go places that are unsafe for humans. Additionally, robotics in education serves as a valuable tool for teaching programming and engineering concepts.

AI Hardware and Software

AI Processors

AI processors are specialized hardware designed to efficiently process AI workloads, particularly those involving neural networks and machine learning algorithms. These processors are optimized for parallel processing, high-speed computation, and handling large volumes of data. Examples include Graphics Processing Units (GPUs), Tensor Processing Units (TPUs), and Field-Programmable Gate Arrays (FPGAs).

AI Software Platforms

AI software platforms provide tools and frameworks to facilitate the development of AI models. These platforms often include pre-built algorithms, data preprocessing tools, and model training and deployment capabilities. Popular AI software platforms include TensorFlow, PyTorch, and Keras, which are widely used for building and training deep learning models.

Cloud-based AI Services

Cloud-based AI services offer AI capabilities as a service over the internet, allowing users to access powerful AI tools without the need for significant hardware investments. These services provide APIs for various AI tasks such as speech recognition, text analysis, image processing, and machine learning model hosting. Major cloud providers like Amazon Web Services, Microsoft Azure, and Google Cloud Platform offer a range of AI services that enable businesses to integrate AI into their operations with greater ease and flexibility.

Review Questions

1. What is the primary difference between Machine Learning and Deep Learning?
2. Which of the following is NOT a component of Natural Language Processing?
3. What is the primary function of Computer Vision in AI?
4. Which of the following is NOT a type of robot?
5. What is the role of AI Processors in AI Hardware?
6. What are the different types of Machine Learning and how are they used in business?
7. What is Natural Language Processing and what are its main components?
8. How does Computer Vision differ from Robotics in terms of their applications in business?

CHAPTER 3

AI Applications in Business

Artificial Intelligence (AI) has revolutionized the way businesses approach marketing. AI-powered marketing strategies enable companies to analyze vast amounts of data to identify patterns and insights that were previously undetectable. By leveraging machine learning algorithms, businesses can predict consumer behavior, personalize marketing messages, and optimize the timing and placement of ads. AI tools can also automate repetitive tasks, such as A/B testing and campaign analysis, freeing up marketers to focus on creative and strategic initiatives.

One of the most significant advantages of AI in marketing is its ability to process and interpret big data to make informed decisions. For instance, AI can sift through social media interactions to understand consumer sentiment towards a brand or product. This insight allows businesses to tailor their marketing efforts to align with consumer preferences, resulting in more effective campaigns and a higher return on investment

(ROI).

Furthermore, AI-driven marketing strategies can adapt in real-time to changing market conditions. Predictive analytics can forecast future trends, enabling businesses to stay ahead of the curve and adjust their strategies accordingly. As AI continues to evolve, the potential for hyper-personalized and dynamic marketing strategies becomes increasingly attainable for businesses of all sizes.

AI in Content Creation

Content creation is another area where AI has made a significant impact. AI-powered content generation tools can produce written material, from news articles to product descriptions, by learning from existing content and following predefined rules and styles. These tools can save time and resources, allowing businesses to scale their content marketing efforts efficiently.

Additionally, AI can assist in curating content that resonates with specific audience segments. By analyzing user engagement data, AI can suggest topics that are likely to perform well and even help optimize content for search engines (SEO). This targeted approach to content creation ensures that businesses can produce relevant and engaging material that captures the attention of their intended audience.

ChatGPT to enhance SEO efforts and profitability, with diverse strategic approaches:

FAQ Generation:

After creating a blog post, use ChatGPT to generate FAQs related to the content. Insert these FAQs at the end of each post to improve search visibility and user engagement, addressing long-tail queries that your audience might search for.

Reporter AI Implementation:

Leverage ChatGPT to act as a 'Reporter AI,' gathering the latest trends, news, and research in your industry. Use this information to create timely and relevant content that attracts more visitors and positions your site as an authority, boosting your SEO ranking.

Long-Form Content Development:

Utilize ChatGPT to assist in creating comprehensive long-form content that covers topics in depth. Google favors detailed content that provides value to users, which can lead to higher rankings and increased organic traffic.

Content Refreshing:

Periodically update older blog posts with new information using insights generated by ChatGPT. This keeps content fresh and relevant, encouraging Google to re-crawl and possibly re-rank these pages higher.

Keyword Optimization:

Use ChatGPT to identify secondary keywords or semantic variations related to your main topic. Incorporating these naturally into your content can improve your page's relevance for a broader range of search queries.
Meta Description and Title Tag Generation:

Craft unique and compelling meta descriptions and title tags for each page using ChatGPT, incorporating target keywords. Well-written meta tags can improve click-through rates from search engine results pages (SERPs), indirectly boosting SEO performance.

Link Building Outreach:

Generate personalized outreach emails with ChatGPT for link-building campaigns. Tailored emails can increase the likelihood of receiving backlinks from reputable sites, a key factor in SEO ranking.
Voice Search Optimization:

Ask ChatGPT to convert your content into a more conversational tone suitable for voice search queries. As voice search grows, optimizing for natural language can capture this segment of search traffic.
Structured Data Creation:

Utilize ChatGPT to help generate structured data (schema markup) for your web pages. Structured data helps search engines understand and index your content more effectively, potentially enhancing visibility in rich snippets.

Social Media Snippets:

Create engaging social media snippets or posts from your main content with ChatGPT. Sharing these snippets across social platforms can drive social signals and traffic back to your site, indirectly benefiting SEO.

By diversifying the use of ChatGPT across these various strategies, businesses can significantly enhance their content's SEO performance, driving higher organic traffic and ultimately boosting profitability through increased visibility and engagement.

AI in Customer Segmentation

Customer segmentation is the process of dividing a business's customer base into distinct groups that share similar characteristics. AI enhances this process by enabling businesses to segment their customers with unprecedented precision. By analyzing customer data, AI can identify patterns and group customers based on various factors, such as purchasing behavior, demographics, and online activity.

This granular approach to segmentation allows for highly personalized marketing campaigns. Businesses can tailor their messaging and offers to meet the specific needs and preferences of each segment, resulting in increased customer engagement and loyalty. AI-driven customer segmentation is a powerful tool for businesses looking to maximize the effectiveness of their marketing efforts.

AI in Sales

AI in Lead Generation

Lead generation is a critical component of the sales process, and AI has transformed how businesses identify and attract potential customers. AI algorithms can analyze data from various sources, such as website visits, social media interactions, and past purchase history, to identify potential leads. These algorithms can score leads based on their likelihood to convert, enabling sales teams to prioritize their efforts and focus on the most promising prospects.

AI can also automate the initial outreach to potential leads through personalized emails or social media messages. By using natural language processing (NLP), AI can craft messages that are not only relevant to the lead's interests but also written in a way that feels personal and engaging. This automation helps businesses to increase their lead generation efforts without a corresponding increase in labor costs.

AI in Sales Forecasting

Sales forecasting is essential for businesses to plan their inventory, cash flow, and growth strategies. AI enhances sales forecasting by analyzing historical sales data, market trends, and other external factors to predict future sales with a high degree of accuracy. Machine learning models can continuously learn from new data, refining their predictions over time.

Accurate sales forecasts enable businesses to make informed decisions about production, staffing, and budget allocation. AI-driven forecasting tools can also identify potential risks and opportunities, allowing businesses to proactively adjust their strategies in response to predicted market changes.

AI in Customer Relationship Management

Customer Relationship Management (CRM) systems have traditionally been used to store and manage customer data. With the integration of AI, these systems have become more intelligent and proactive. AI can analyze customer interactions and provide sales representatives with insights and recommendations on how to best engage with each customer.

AI can also predict customer needs and suggest upsell or cross-sell opportunities, increasing the value of each customer relationship. By providing a personalized experience, AI-driven CRM systems help businesses build stronger, more profitable relationships with their customers.

Test Your Knowledge

Let's see how well you understood the role of AI in Customer Relationship Management (CRM). Try to answer the following questions:

1. What is the traditional use of CRM systems in business?
2. How has the integration of AI changed the functionality of CRM systems?
3. What kind of insights can AI provide to sales representatives through CRM systems?
4. How does AI in CRM systems help in upselling or cross-selling?
5. How does AI-driven CRM contribute to building stronger and more profitable relationships with customers?

Check your answers at the end of the chapter. Remember, understanding these concepts will help you leverage AI in business effectively!

AI in Customer Service

AI Chatbots

AI chatbots are virtual assistants that can interact with customers in real-time, providing instant support and resolving inquiries. These chatbots use NLP to understand customer queries and respond appropriately. They can handle a wide range of tasks, from answering frequently asked questions to guiding customers through complex processes.

The use of AI chatbots in customer service not only improves the customer experience by providing immediate assistance but also reduces the workload on human customer service representatives. This allows businesses to scale their customer service operations without a proportional increase in staff.

AI in Customer Support Automation

Beyond chatbots, AI can automate various aspects of customer support. For example, AI can categorize incoming support tickets based on their content and route them to the appropriate department or representative. This automation speeds up the resolution process and ensures that customers receive help from the most qualified person.

AI can also analyze past support interactions to identify common issues and develop solutions proactively. By doing so, businesses can address problems before they affect a large number of customers, improving overall customer satisfaction.

AI in Personalized Customer Experience

Personalization is key to creating a memorable customer experience. AI enables businesses to personalize the customer experience at scale by analyzing individual customer data and delivering content, recommendations, and support that are tailored to each customer's preferences and behavior.

For instance, e-commerce websites can use AI to recommend products that a customer is likely to be interested in based on their browsing and purchase history. This level of personalization not only enhances the shopping experience but also increases the likelihood of conversion and repeat business.

Think & Reflect

Consider the following:

1. Think about the last time you shopped online. Did you notice any personalized recommendations? How did these recommendations influence your shopping behavior?
2. Can you think of any other ways AI could be used to personalize the customer experience? How might

these applications benefit both the customer and the business?

3. Consider the ethical implications of using AI to analyze individual customer data. What measures could businesses take to ensure they respect customer privacy while still leveraging the benefits of AI?

AI in Operations and Logistics

AI in Supply Chain Optimization

Supply chain optimization is crucial for businesses to ensure efficiency and reduce costs. AI can analyze data from various points in the supply chain to identify bottlenecks and predict potential disruptions. By using AI to optimize routing, inventory levels, and supplier relationships, businesses can create a more resilient and responsive supply chain.

AI can also facilitate demand forecasting, which is essential for maintaining optimal inventory levels. By predicting future demand with high accuracy, businesses can avoid overstocking or stockouts, both of which can be costly.

AI in Inventory Management

Inventory management is another area where AI can have a significant impact. AI systems can continuously monitor inventory levels and automatically reorder products when stocks fall below a certain threshold. This automation ensures that businesses always have the right amount of inventory on hand to meet customer demand without tying up too much capital in unsold goods.

Additionally, AI can analyze sales data to identify trends and seasonality, allowing businesses to adjust their inventory management strategies accordingly. This proactive approach to inventory management helps businesses reduce waste and improve profitability.

AI in Delivery and Logistics

In the realm of delivery and logistics, AI can optimize delivery routes to minimize travel time and fuel consumption. By analyzing traffic patterns, weather conditions, and delivery windows, AI can determine the most efficient routes for delivery vehicles. This optimization leads to faster delivery times, reduced operational costs, and a lower environmental impact.

AI can also predict delivery issues before they occur, allowing businesses to proactively communicate with customers and manage their expectations. This level of service can significantly enhance customer satisfaction and loyalty.

AI in Human Resources

AI in Recruitment

Recruitment is a time-consuming process that AI can streamline significantly. AI-powered recruitment tools can scan resumes and applications to identify the most qualified candidates based on predefined criteria. This automation speeds up the initial screening process and helps reduce unconscious bias in hiring decisions.

AI can also assist in passive candidate sourcing by identifying potential candidates who may not be actively seeking a new job but possess the skills and experience required for a role. By leveraging AI in recruitment, businesses can improve the efficiency and effectiveness of their hiring processes.

AI in Employee Engagement

Employee engagement is critical for retaining top talent and maintaining high productivity. AI can analyze employee feedback and engagement data to identify trends and areas for improvement. AI-driven tools can also provide personalized recommendations for employee development and career progression, fostering a more engaged and motivated workforce.

Furthermore, AI can facilitate personalized learning experiences by recommending training and development opportunities tailored to each employee's skills and career goals. This personalized approach to employee development can lead to a more skilled and adaptable workforce.

AI in Performance Management

Performance management is essential for ensuring that employees are meeting their goals and contributing to the company's success. AI can assist in this process by providing managers with data-driven insights into employee performance. AI tools can track key performance indicators (KPIs) and highlight areas where employees excel or need improvement.

AI can also help set realistic and challenging performance goals based on historical data and predictive analytics. By using AI to inform performance management, businesses can create a more objective and effective system for evaluating and improving employee performance.

AI in Financial Management

AI in Fraud Detection

Fraud detection is a critical concern for businesses, and AI has proven to be an invaluable tool in identifying and preventing fraudulent activities. AI systems can analyze transaction data in real-time to detect anomalies that may indicate fraud. These systems learn from each transaction, becoming more adept at identifying fraudulent patterns over time.

By implementing AI in fraud detection, businesses can reduce the risk of financial loss and protect their reputation. AI-driven fraud detection systems can also adapt to new types of fraud, ensuring that businesses remain one step ahead of fraudsters.

AI in Risk Assessment

Risk assessment is essential for making informed business decisions. AI can analyze market data, economic indicators, and internal metrics to identify potential risks to a business's financial health. By using AI to assess risk, businesses can take proactive measures to mitigate those risks and protect their bottom line.

AI can also assist in credit risk assessment by analyzing the creditworthiness of customers or partners. This analysis helps businesses make more informed decisions about extending credit and managing their financial relationships.

AI in Financial Forecasting

Financial forecasting is crucial for planning and budgeting. AI enhances the accuracy of financial forecasts by analyzing historical financial data and identifying trends that may impact future performance. AI-driven forecasting tools can also incorporate external data, such as market conditions and regulatory changes, to provide a comprehensive view of a business's financial future.

With AI in financial forecasting, businesses can make more strategic decisions about investments, growth opportunities, and resource allocation. The ability to forecast financial outcomes with greater precision allows businesses to navigate uncertainty with confidence.

Review Questions

1. How can AI be used in marketing?
2. What is the role of AI in sales?
3. How does AI contribute to customer service?
4. What is the application of AI in operations and logistics?
5. How is AI used in financial management?
6. How does AI contribute to marketing strategies?
7. What are some applications of AI in operations and logistics?
8. How can AI be utilized in the field of human resources?

CHAPTER 4

AI and Marketing Strategies

AI and Making Money with ChatGPT at Home:

* * *

Entrepreneurs can leverage ChatGPT, in several innovative ways to generate income from home. Here's how:

1. Content Creation and Enhancement

Blogging and Article Writing: Use ChatGPT to generate ideas, outlines, or even draft entire articles for a blog. Tailor content to niche markets with high search traffic but low competition to attract a dedicated readership that can be monetized through ads, affiliate marketing, or sponsored content.

E-book Writing: Draft e-books on trending topics or evergreen subjects. ChatGPT can help research, outline, and write sections of e-books that can be sold on platforms like Amazon Kindle Direct Publishing.

2. Digital Marketing Services

Social Media Management: Develop social media content strategies, create engaging posts, or write compelling ad copy with ChatGPT's assistance. Offer these services to businesses looking to enhance their online presence.

Email Marketing Campaigns: Use ChatGPT to craft personalized email marketing campaigns for businesses or your projects. Effective email sequences can improve customer retention and increase sales.

3. Online Education and Courses

Course Creation: Design educational content and courses on subjects you're knowledgeable about. ChatGPT can help structure your course, create lesson plans, and even draft course material that can be sold through platforms like Udemy or Teachable.

Tutoring and Coaching: Provide tutoring in areas of your expertise. Use ChatGPT to develop teaching materials, practice questions, and explanatory content to enhance your tutoring sessions.

4. E-commerce and Dropshipping

Product Descriptions: If you run an e-commerce or dropshipping business, use ChatGPT to write creative and persuasive product descriptions that can boost your sales.

Customer Service Automation: Implement ChatGPT-driven chatbots on your e-commerce site to handle customer inquiries, provide product recommendations, and support, thereby improving the customer experience and potentially increasing sales.

5. Software and App Development
App Development: Utilize ChatGPT for brainstorming app ideas, writing app descriptions, and even coding assistance. Apps can be monetized through in-app purchases, subscriptions, or ads.

Web Development: Offer web development services by leveraging ChatGPT for coding assistance, content creation for websites, and SEO optimization strategies.

6. Affiliate Marketing
Niche Research: Use ChatGPT to identify profitable niches for affiliate marketing. Then, create content around those niches and incorporate affiliate links.

7. Consultancy Services
Business Consulting: If you have expertise in a specific industry, offer consulting services. ChatGPT can help prepare reports, presentations, and market analyses to support your consultancy work.

Implementing These Ideas

Continuous Learning: Stay informed about the latest trends in your chosen area of entrepreneurship. Use ChatGPT to research articles, studies, and news.
Visit my blog for new ideas: www.christopherdessi.com

Networking: Use LinkedIn and other professional networks to connect with potential clients or partners. ChatGPT can help craft personalized outreach messages.

By incorporating ChatGPT into these entrepreneurial endeavors, you can streamline your workflow, enhance the quality of your output, and explore new avenues for income generation—all from the comfort of your home.

AI in Digital Marketing

AI in SEO

Search Engine Optimization (SEO) is a critical component of digital marketing that involves optimizing web content to rank higher on search engine results pages (SERPs). AI has revolutionized SEO by enabling more efficient keyword research, content optimization, and analysis of search engine algorithms. AI tools can predict which keywords will become more popular and how users interact with content, allowing businesses to stay ahead of trends.

Additionally, AI-driven SEO tools can analyze vast amounts of data to understand search engine ranking factors better. They can suggest changes to website structure, content, and backlinks to improve visibility. AI also helps in creating more personalized content strategies by understanding user intent and delivering content that matches their needs.

AI in Social Media Marketing

Social media platforms are fertile ground for AI applications in marketing. AI algorithms can analyze social media trends, track brand mentions, and understand consumer sentiment. This information helps marketers to tailor their content and campaigns to resonate with their target audience better. AI-powered tools can also automate the posting of content at optimal times to maximize engagement and reach.

AI is also used in social media advertising to target users more precisely. By analyzing user data, AI can identify patterns and preferences, enabling highly targeted advertising that is more likely to convert. Furthermore, AI can monitor the performance of social media campaigns in real-time, providing insights that can be used to adjust strategies on the fly.

AI in Email Marketing

Email marketing remains a powerful tool for businesses, and AI has made it even more effective. AI can personalize email content for each recipient, increasing the likelihood of engagement. By analyzing past interactions, purchase history, and browsing behavior, AI can determine the best products, services, or content to feature in emails to individual customers.

AI also optimizes email campaign performance by determining the best times to send emails, segmenting email lists more effectively, and testing different email subject lines and content to see what performs best. This level of personalization and optimization leads to higher open rates, click-through rates, and conversions.

AI in Content Marketing

AI in Content Creation

Content is king in the digital marketing world, and AI is the power behind the throne. AI-driven content creation tools can generate articles, reports, and even creative stories. These tools use natural language processing (NLP) and machine learning to produce content that is coherent, relevant, and tailored to specific audiences.

While AI-generated content is not yet indistinguishable from human-written content, it is increasingly being used to create initial drafts or to generate ideas that can be refined by human writers. This can save time and resources, allowing content creators to focus on strategy and storytelling.

AI in Content Curation

Content curation is the process of gathering and presenting content from various sources. AI enhances this process by quickly analyzing and sorting through large volumes of content to find the most relevant and high-quality pieces. This allows marketers to provide their audience with a curated selection of content that is most likely to interest them, without the need for time-consuming manual research.

AI systems can also learn from user interactions, continuously improving the relevance of the content they curate. This personalized approach keeps audiences engaged and can help establish a brand as a thought leader in its field.

AI in Content Distribution

Distributing content effectively is as important as creating it. AI helps in identifying the best channels and platforms for content distribution based on audience preferences and behaviors.
It can also automate the distribution process, ensuring that content is shared consistently across all selected channels.

AI-driven analytics can track the performance of distributed content across different platforms, providing insights into what types of content work best on each channel. This data-driven approach helps marketers refine their content distribution strategies for maximum impact.

Quick Facts & Statistics

AI in Marketing

Artificial Intelligence (AI) is revolutionizing the marketing industry. Here are some interesting facts and statistics:

AI in Content Distribution

AI is also making a significant impact in content distribution. Here's how:

AI in Advertising

AI in Ad Targeting

Ad targeting has been transformed by AI's ability to analyze vast amounts of data to identify the most promising prospects for a campaign. AI algorithms can process demographic information, online behavior, and purchasing history to create detailed profiles of ideal customers. This enables highly targeted advertising that is more likely to result in conversions.

AI can also dynamically adjust ad targeting based on real-time data, ensuring that ads are always reaching the most relevant audience. This level of precision in ad targeting was previously unattainable and represents a significant advancement in advertising efficiency.

AI in Ad Optimization

Once ads are live, AI continues to play a crucial role in optimizing their performance. AI algorithms can test different ad variations, including images, headlines, and calls to action, to determine which combinations perform best. This process, known as A/B testing or split testing, can be automated and scaled by AI, leading to continuous improvement in ad effectiveness.

AI can also manage ad spend across different platforms, reallocating budgets to the most successful campaigns and reducing spend on underperforming ads. This ensures that marketing budgets are used as effectively as possible to achieve the best return on investment (ROI).

AI in Ad Performance Analysis

Analyzing ad performance is essential for understanding the success of marketing campaigns. AI provides detailed insights into ad performance metrics such as click-through rates, conversion rates, and cost per acquisition. By processing this data, AI can identify trends and patterns that may not be immediately apparent to human analysts.

These insights can inform future ad campaigns, allowing marketers to replicate successful strategies and avoid past mistakes. AI-driven performance analysis is a powerful tool for refining advertising efforts and maximizing the impact of every marketing dollar spent.

AI in Customer Journey Mapping

AI in Customer Segmentation

Understanding the customer journey is vital for creating effective marketing strategies. AI enhances customer segmentation by analyzing data points across the customer lifecycle to group individuals with similar behaviors, preferences, and needs. This granular segmentation allows for more targeted and personalized marketing efforts.

AI can uncover hidden patterns in customer data that might be missed by traditional segmentation methods. This leads to a deeper understanding of customer segments and the ability to tailor marketing messages that resonate with each unique group.

AI in Personalization

Personalization is the cornerstone of modern marketing, and AI takes it to a new level. By leveraging data on individual customer preferences and behaviors, AI can create personalized experiences across various touchpoints. This includes personalized product recommendations, customized website experiences, and tailored communication.

The ability of AI to process and act on data in real-time means that personalization can occur at the moment, providing customers with relevant experiences when they are most engaged. This level of personalization not only improves customer satisfaction but also drives higher conversion rates.

AI in Predictive Analytics

Predictive analytics uses historical data to forecast future events, and AI enhances this process by making predictions more accurate and actionable. In marketing, AI-driven predictive analytics can anticipate customer needs, predict purchasing behavior, and identify potential churn risks.

Marketers can use these insights to proactively address customer concerns, offer timely promotions, and retain customers at risk of leaving. Predictive analytics powered by AI helps businesses stay one step ahead of the market and their competition.

Test Your Knowledge

Let's see how well you've understood the concepts of AI in Predictive Analytics!

1. What is predictive analytics and how does AI enhance this process?
2. How can marketers use AI-driven predictive analytics in their strategies?
3. What are some benefits of using predictive analytics powered by AI in business?

Remember, understanding these concepts is key to leveraging AI in your business strategies. Keep revising and practicing!

AI in Marketing Analytics

AI in Market Research

Market research is essential for understanding the competitive landscape and consumer trends. AI accelerates this process by quickly analyzing large datasets from various sources, including social media, customer reviews, and market reports. This analysis can reveal insights into consumer behavior, emerging trends, and market opportunities.

AI can also identify correlations and causations within the

data that may not be immediately obvious, providing a more nuanced understanding of the market. This level of insight is invaluable for developing effective marketing strategies.

AI in Sentiment Analysis

Sentiment analysis is the process of determining the emotional tone behind a body of text. AI excels at sentiment analysis by using NLP to understand the context and nuances of language used in customer feedback, social media posts, and other text-based communications.

This allows businesses to gauge public sentiment towards their brand, products, or services. Understanding sentiment helps marketers to adjust their messaging, address customer concerns, and capitalize on positive sentiment to enhance brand reputation.

AI in Marketing ROI Measurement

Measuring the ROI of marketing campaigns is crucial for understanding their effectiveness. AI streamlines this process by tracking and attributing conversions to specific marketing activities. It can also factor in complex variables such as customer lifetime value and brand equity to provide a more comprehensive view of ROI.

With AI, marketers can quickly identify which campaigns are driving results and allocate resources accordingly. This data-driven approach ensures that marketing efforts are focused on the most profitable activities.

Future of AI in Marketing

Emerging AI Technologies in Marketing

The future of AI in marketing is bright, with new technologies emerging that will further transform the field. Advances in AI such as generative adversarial networks (GANs) are beginning to be used for creating highly realistic images and videos, which can be used in advertising and content creation. AI is also being integrated with augmented reality (AR) and virtual reality (VR) to create immersive marketing experiences.

Another exciting development is the use of AI for real-time personalization at scale. This technology allows businesses to deliver personalized experiences to thousands or even millions of customers simultaneously, something that was previously impossible.

Ethical Considerations in AI Marketing

As AI becomes more prevalent in marketing, ethical considerations must be addressed. Issues such as data privacy, consent, and transparency are at the forefront of discussions around AI ethics. Marketers must ensure that they use AI responsibly, respecting customer privacy and being transparent about how customer data is used.

There is also a risk of AI perpetuating biases if the data it is trained on is not diverse and representative. Marketers must be vigilant in monitoring AI systems for bias and take steps to mitigate any issues that arise.

AI in Marketing: Opportunities and Challenges

AI presents numerous opportunities for marketers to engage with customers more effectively, create more impactful campaigns, and measure results with unprecedented precision. However, there are also challenges, including the need for skilled personnel to manage AI systems, the potential for AI to replace jobs, and the ongoing need to keep AI systems up to date with the latest algorithms and data.

Despite these challenges, the potential benefits of AI in marketing are too significant to ignore. Businesses that embrace AI will be well-positioned to lead in their markets and deliver exceptional customer experiences.

Review Questions

1. How is AI used in SEO?
2. What is the role of AI in content curation?

3. How does AI contribute to ad optimization?
4. What is the purpose of AI in customer segmentation?
5. What is one of the future challenges of AI in marketing?
6. How does AI contribute to the optimization of email marketing strategies?
7. What role does AI play in content curation and distribution?
8. How can AI be used in ad performance analysis?

CHAPTER 5

AI in Customer Service

AI Chatbots in Customer Service

AI chatbots are software applications designed to simulate conversation with human users, especially over the internet. They are integrated with artificial intelligence (AI) technologies, including natural language processing (NLP) and machine learning (ML), which enable them to understand, process, and respond to human language in a way that is both natural and effective. AI chatbots can be deployed on various platforms such as websites, messaging apps, and social media channels, providing instant and automated customer support.

The sophistication of AI chatbots can vary greatly. Some are rule-based systems that provide pre-defined responses to specific commands or questions, while others use more advanced machine learning algorithms to learn from interactions and improve their responses over time. The most advanced chatbots are capable of understanding context, managing nuanced conversations, and even expressing personality traits to make the interaction more engaging for users.

Benefits of AI Chatbots

AI chatbots offer numerous benefits to businesses, particularly in the realm of customer service. One of the primary advantages is their ability to provide 24/7 support, which ensures that customer inquiries are addressed at any time of day without the need for human intervention. This round-the-clock availability can significantly enhance customer satisfaction and loyalty.

Another benefit is the scalability of AI chatbots. They can handle a vast number of conversations simultaneously, which can help businesses manage high volumes of customer interactions during peak times without compromising the quality of service. Additionally, chatbots can reduce operational costs by automating routine inquiries, allowing human customer service representatives to focus on more complex and high-value tasks.

AI chatbots also contribute to the collection of valuable customer data. Each interaction can be analyzed to gain insights into customer preferences, behavior, and feedback. This data can be used to personalize future interactions and inform business decisions, leading to improved customer experiences and product offerings.

Case Studies of AI Chatbots

Several companies have successfully implemented AI chatbots to enhance their customer service. For example, a major airline introduced a chatbot to handle common customer queries regarding flight status, booking, and baggage policies. The chatbot was able to reduce the volume of calls to the customer service center by 40%, leading to cost savings and increased customer satisfaction.

Another case study involves a retail company that deployed a chatbot to assist customers with product selection and checkout processes. The chatbot's integration with the company's e-commerce platform allowed it to provide personalized recommendations based on the customer's browsing history and preferences. As a result, the company saw a 25% increase in online sales and a significant improvement in customer engagement.

AI in Customer Support Automation

Understanding Customer Support Automation

Customer support automation involves the use of AI technologies to automate various aspects of the customer service process. This includes the use of chatbots for handling inquiries, as well as automated ticketing systems, self-service knowledge bases, and automated responses to emails and social media messages. The goal of customer support automation is to streamline the service process, reduce response times, and improve the overall efficiency of customer support operations.

Automation can be applied to both front-end customer interactions and back-end processes. For instance, AI can help categorize and route support tickets to the appropriate department or representative based on the content of the inquiry. It can also assist in prioritizing tickets based on urgency or customer value, ensuring that critical issues are addressed promptly.

Benefits of Customer Support Automation

The benefits of customer support automation are manifold. By automating routine tasks, businesses can reduce the workload on human agents, allowing them to concentrate on more complex issues that require a personal touch. This not only improves the efficiency of the support team but also enhances job satisfaction among employees by reducing the monotony of repetitive tasks.

Automation also contributes to a more consistent customer service experience. Automated systems can provide uniform responses to frequently asked questions, ensuring that all customers receive accurate and up-to-date information. This consistency helps to build trust and reliability in the brand.

Furthermore, customer support automation can lead to faster resolution times. Automated systems can quickly sort through and respond to simple inquiries, reducing the backlog of support tickets and enabling human agents to address more complex issues in a timely manner.

Case Studies of Customer Support Automation

A telecommunications company implemented an AI-driven support automation system to manage its customer inquiries. The system was able to categorize and route tickets with high accuracy, leading to a 30% reduction in average resolution time. The company also reported higher customer satisfaction scores due to the quicker and more accurate responses provided by the automated system.

In another instance, a financial services firm used AI to power its self-service knowledge base. The AI was trained to understand complex financial queries and provide clear, concise answers. This allowed customers to resolve many of their issues without the need for direct interaction with a service agent, resulting in a 50% decrease in inbound support requests.

AI in Personalized Customer Experience

Understanding Personalized Customer Experience

Personalized customer experience refers to the practice of tailoring interactions and services to meet the individual needs and preferences of each customer. AI plays a crucial role in enabling this personalization by analyzing customer data, such as past purchases, browsing behavior, and interaction history, to deliver a more relevant and engaging experience.

AI technologies can segment customers into distinct groups based on their behavior and preferences, allowing businesses to target them with personalized messages, offers, and recommendations. This level of personalization can significantly enhance the customer's experience, leading to increased loyalty and higher conversion rates.

Benefits of Personalized Customer Experience

The benefits of a personalized customer experience are extensive. Customers are more likely to engage with a brand that recognizes their individual needs and provides relevant content and recommendations. This relevance can lead to a deeper emotional connection with the brand and a greater likelihood of repeat business.

Personalization also allows businesses to stand out in a crowded market. By offering a unique and tailored experience, companies can differentiate themselves from competitors and create a competitive advantage.

Additionally, personalization can lead to more efficient marketing spend. By targeting customers with offers and content that are more likely to resonate with them, businesses can achieve higher returns on investment for their marketing efforts.

Case Studies of Personalized Customer Experience

A leading e-commerce platform used AI to personalize the shopping experience for its customers. By analyzing customer data, the AI was able to provide personalized product recommendations, which led to a 35% increase in average order value. The platform also used AI to personalize email marketing campaigns, resulting in a 20% higher click-through rate compared to non-personalized emails.

Another example comes from a hotel chain that implemented AI to personalize the guest experience. The AI system used data from previous stays to customize room settings, such as temperature and lighting, according to guest preferences. This attention to detail significantly improved guest satisfaction and loyalty.

Did You Know?

Artificial Intelligence is not just limited to providing personalized experiences in e-commerce and hospitality industries. It's being used across a wide range of sectors for enhancing customer service. Here are a few more examples:

These are just a few examples. The potential of AI in enhancing customer service and creating personalized experiences is vast and still largely untapped.

AI in Customer Feedback Analysis

Understanding Customer Feedback Analysis

Customer feedback analysis involves the examination and interpretation of feedback provided by customers to gain insights into their satisfaction, preferences, and expectations. AI enhances this process by using natural language processing to understand and categorize feedback from various sources, such as surveys, reviews, social media, and direct customer interactions.

AI can identify patterns and trends in customer feedback, which can be used to inform product development, service improvements, and customer relationship strategies. It can also detect sentiment, allowing businesses to understand the emotions behind customer feedback and respond appropriately.

Benefits of Customer Feedback Analysis

The benefits of using AI for customer feedback analysis are significant. AI can process large volumes of feedback data quickly and accurately, providing real-time insights that can be used to make informed decisions. This rapid analysis enables businesses to be more responsive to customer needs and market changes.

AI-driven feedback analysis also helps businesses identify areas for improvement and prioritize actions based on the impact on customer satisfaction. By understanding customer sentiment, companies can address negative feedback proactively and reinforce positive experiences to build brand loyalty.

Moreover, AI can uncover hidden insights that may not be immediately apparent through manual analysis. These insights can lead to innovative solutions and strategies that drive customer satisfaction and business growth.

Case Studies of Customer Feedback Analysis

A restaurant chain utilized AI to analyze customer reviews and feedback across various platforms. The AI system identified common issues related to service speed and food quality. By addressing these issues, the chain saw a 15% improvement in customer satisfaction scores within six months.

In the healthcare sector, a hospital implemented an AI system to analyze patient feedback. The AI identified a need for better communication regarding treatment plans and aftercare. The hospital used these insights to train staff and develop new communication protocols, leading to higher patient satisfaction and better health outcomes.

AI in Customer Retention

Understanding Customer Retention

Customer retention refers to the ability of a business to retain its customers over time. It is a critical aspect of business success, as retaining existing customers is often more cost-effective than acquiring new ones. AI can play a pivotal role in customer retention by predicting which customers are at risk of churning and by enabling personalized retention strategies.

AI systems can analyze customer behavior, transaction history, and engagement levels to identify patterns that may indicate a risk of churn. Once at-risk customers are identified, AI can help tailor retention efforts, such as targeted offers or personalized communications, to re-engage these customers and address their concerns.

Benefits of AI in Customer Retention

The use of AI in customer retention offers several benefits. By predicting churn, businesses can take proactive measures to retain customers, which can lead to increased customer lifetime value and reduced marketing costs. Personalized retention strategies can also enhance customer satisfaction and loyalty, as customers feel valued and understood by the brand.

AI-driven retention efforts can also provide a more efficient use of resources. Instead of applying broad retention strategies to all customers, businesses can focus their efforts on those who are most likely to churn, resulting in a more targeted and effective approach.

Case Studies of AI in Customer Retention

A mobile phone carrier used AI to analyze customer usage patterns and service interactions. The AI identified customers who were likely to cancel their service and triggered personalized retention offers, such as discounts on upgrades or tailored service plans. This approach reduced churn by 20% within the first year of implementation.

An online streaming service utilized AI to recommend content based on individual viewing habits. By keeping customers engaged with relevant content, the service was able to maintain a high retention rate and increase the average subscription length by several months.

Quotes

"The future of business is social." - Barry Libert, CEO of OpenMatters and a pioneer in AI and machine learning in business.

"The only way to win at content marketing is for the reader to say, 'This was written specifically for me.'" - Jamie Turner, an internationally recognized author, speaker and CEO with a deep understanding of AI's role in marketing.

"The best way to predict the future is to create it." - Peter Drucker, a renowned management consultant, educator, and author, often associated with the concept of 'knowledge work'.

"Artificial Intelligence, deep learning, machine learning — whatever you're doing if you don't understand it — learn it. Because otherwise you're going to be a dinosaur within 3 years." - Mark Cuban, an American entrepreneur and investor who has been a vocal advocate for the importance of AI in business.

Future of AI in Customer Service

Emerging AI Technologies in Customer Service

The future of AI in customer service is promising, with new technologies emerging that have the potential to further transform the industry. One such technology is voice recognition, which can enable more natural and intuitive interactions with AI systems. Another is emotion AI, which can detect and respond to the emotional state of customers, providing a more empathetic service experience.

Advances in machine learning algorithms will also allow AI systems to become more accurate and efficient in understanding and responding to customer needs. Additionally, the integration of AI with other technologies, such as augmented reality (AR) and virtual reality (VR), could lead to innovative customer service solutions that offer immersive and interactive experiences.

Ethical Considerations in AI Customer Service

As AI continues to play a larger role in customer service, ethical considerations must be addressed. Issues such as data privacy, transparency, and bias in AI algorithms are of particular concern. Businesses must ensure that they use customer data responsibly and that AI systems provide fair and unbiased service to all customers.

Transparency is also crucial, as customers should be aware when they are interacting with an AI system and have the option to speak with a human agent if desired. Companies must also be accountable for the actions of their AI systems and have processes in place to address any issues that arise.

AI in Customer Service: Opportunities and Challenges

The opportunities presented by AI in customer service are vast.

AI can help businesses provide more personalized, efficient, and effective service, leading to higher customer satisfaction and loyalty. However, challenges such as ensuring the quality of AI interactions, maintaining customer trust, and managing the impact on employment must be carefully managed.

Businesses must also stay abreast of technological advancements and continuously evaluate and update their AI systems to meet changing customer expectations. By balancing the opportunities with the challenges, companies can leverage AI to create a competitive advantage and drive business success.

Review Questions

1. What is one of the main benefits of AI chatbots in customer service?
2. What is a key advantage of AI in customer support automation?
3. How does AI contribute to personalized customer experience?

4. What is a significant benefit of AI in customer feedback analysis?
5. How can AI contribute to customer retention?
6. What are the benefits of using AI chatbots in customer service?
7. How does AI contribute to personalized customer experience?
8. What are the ethical considerations in AI customer service?

CHAPTER 6

AI in Financial Management

AI in Financial Planning

Financial planning is a critical aspect of business management, involving the allocation of financial resources to meet the strategic goals of a company. With the advent of artificial intelligence (AI), financial planning has been revolutionized. AI in financial planning refers to the use of machine learning algorithms, data analytics, and predictive modeling to enhance the financial decision-making process. These technologies can process vast amounts of data at incredible speeds, identify patterns, and provide insights that were previously unattainable through traditional methods.

AI systems can analyze market trends, predict future financial scenarios, and provide recommendations for budget allocation, investment strategies, and cost-saving measures. By leveraging AI, businesses can create more accurate financial forecasts, optimize their financial operations, and make informed decisions that align with their long-term objectives.

Benefits of AI in Financial Planning

The benefits of incorporating AI into financial planning are manifold. Firstly, AI enhances accuracy in financial forecasting by considering a broader range of variables and data points. This leads to more reliable predictions about future market conditions and financial outcomes. Secondly, AI-driven financial planning can significantly reduce the time and effort required for data analysis, allowing financial planners to focus on strategic decision-making rather than manual calculations.

Another benefit is the ability of AI to identify opportunities for cost reduction and revenue enhancement by analyzing spending patterns and identifying inefficiencies. Additionally, AI can help in scenario planning by simulating various financial conditions and outcomes, enabling companies to prepare for different market situations. Lastly, AI can improve risk management by predicting potential financial risks and suggesting mitigation strategies.

Case Studies of AI in Financial Planning

A notable case study involves a multinational corporation that implemented an AI-powered financial planning system. The system was able to analyze historical financial data, market trends, and economic indicators to forecast future revenues and expenses with a high degree of accuracy. As a result, the company was able to adjust its financial strategy proactively, leading to a significant increase in profitability.

Another case study features a financial technology startup that developed an AI-based personal financial advisor. The platform uses machine learning to provide personalized financial advice to users, helping them to manage their investments, savings, and expenditures more effectively. The AI advisor continuously learns from the user's financial behavior and market conditions to offer tailored recommendations.

Quick Facts & Statistics

Artificial Intelligence in Financial Management:

AI in Financial Planning:

AI in Personal Financial Advisory:

AI in Risk Management

Understanding AI in Risk Management

Risk management is a crucial component of financial management, involving the identification, assessment, and prioritization of potential financial risks. AI has transformed risk management by enabling businesses to predict and quantify risks with greater precision. AI systems can process complex datasets, including historical financial information, real-time market data, and global economic indicators, to identify potential risks that could impact a company's financial health.

These AI systems can also simulate various risk scenarios and evaluate the potential impact on the company's financials. By doing so, businesses can develop robust risk mitigation strategies and allocate resources more effectively to protect against financial losses.

Benefits of AI in Risk Management

AI offers several benefits in the realm of risk management. It enables continuous monitoring of financial markets and the company's financial activities, allowing for the early detection of potential risks. AI can also provide real-time risk assessments, which is particularly valuable in volatile market conditions where rapid responses are necessary.

Furthermore, AI can enhance the accuracy of risk models by incorporating a wider range of risk factors and data sources. This leads to a more comprehensive understanding of the risk landscape and better-informed risk management decisions. AI also facilitates stress testing and scenario analysis, helping companies to prepare for and respond to adverse financial events.

Case Studies of AI in Risk Management

In one case study, a global bank implemented an AI-driven risk management system that analyzed customer transactions to identify patterns indicative of fraudulent activity. The system significantly reduced the incidence of financial fraud, saving the bank millions of dollars in potential losses.

Another case study involves an insurance company that used AI to assess the risk profiles of potential clients. The AI system evaluated various data points, including credit scores, claims history, and behavioral data, to determine the appropriate insurance premiums. This resulted in a more accurate pricing model and reduced the company's exposure to high-risk clients.

Think & Reflect

Consider the following scenarios:

1. A local bank in your town is considering implementing an AI-driven risk management system similar to the global bank mentioned in the case study. What potential benefits and challenges can you foresee for this local bank?

2. Imagine you are a client of the insurance company that uses AI to assess risk profiles. How would you feel about your personal data, such as credit scores and claims history, being used in this way? What concerns might you have, and how could the company address them?

Reflect on these questions:

- How might the use of AI in risk management change the way businesses operate?
- What ethical considerations come into play when using AI for risk management?
- How could AI potentially be misused in the context of risk management, and what safeguards could be put in place to prevent such misuse?

AI in Fraud Detection

Understanding AI in Fraud Detection

Fraud detection is an area where AI has made significant inroads, providing businesses with powerful tools to combat financial fraud. AI systems in fraud detection use machine learning algorithms to analyze transaction data, recognize patterns, and identify anomalies that may indicate fraudulent activity. These systems can learn from historical fraud cases and adapt to new and evolving fraudulent techniques.

AI-driven fraud detection systems can process large volumes of transactions in real-time, flagging suspicious activities for further investigation. This proactive approach to fraud detection helps businesses minimize losses and maintain the integrity of their financial systems.

Benefits of AI in Fraud Detection

The benefits of using AI for fraud detection are substantial. AI systems can detect fraud with higher accuracy and speed compared to traditional methods, which often rely on rule-based systems that can be easily circumvented by sophisticated fraudsters. AI also reduces the number of false positives, which can be costly and time-consuming to investigate.

Additionally, AI can uncover complex fraud schemes by analyzing relationships and patterns across multiple data sources and transactions. This holistic approach to fraud detection is particularly effective in combating organized financial crime. Moreover, AI systems can adapt and learn from new fraud patterns, ensuring that they remain effective as fraudsters' tactics evolve.

Case Studies of AI in Fraud Detection

A notable case study in this area involves a leading online

retailer that implemented an AI-based fraud detection system. The system analyzed customer transactions and identified fraudulent orders with a high degree of accuracy, leading to a significant reduction in chargebacks and fraud-related losses.

Another case study features a credit card company that used AI to monitor cardholder transactions. The AI system was able to detect unusual spending patterns and alert cardholders to potential fraud in real-time, enhancing customer trust and reducing financial losses due to credit card fraud.

AI in Investment Management

Understanding AI in Investment Management

Investment management is another area where AI has had a profound impact. AI in investment management involves the use of algorithms and data analysis to inform investment decisions and portfolio management. AI systems can analyze market data, financial news, and economic reports to identify investment opportunities and risks.

These systems can also manage investment portfolios by automatically adjusting asset allocations based on market conditions and the investor's risk profile. AI-driven investment management can lead to more dynamic and responsive investment strategies that can outperform traditional, static approaches.

Benefits of AI in Investment Management

AI offers several advantages in investment management. It can process vast amounts of market data to identify trends and insights that human analysts may overlook. AI also enables the execution of high-frequency trades at optimal times, potentially increasing returns. Additionally, AI can provide personalized investment advice to individual investors, taking into account their financial goals and risk tolerance.

AI-driven investment management also allows for the diversification of investment portfolios across a wider range of asset classes and geographies, spreading risk and increasing the potential for returns. Moreover, AI can continuously monitor portfolio performance and make real-time adjustments to align with changing market conditions.

Case Studies of AI in Investment Management

One case study involves a hedge fund that utilized AI algorithms to analyze market sentiment and execute trades based on predictive signals. The fund was able to achieve higher returns compared to its peers by leveraging AI to make data-driven investment decisions.

Another case study features a robo-advisor platform that provides automated investment management services to clients. The platform uses AI to create customized investment portfolios for clients and manages these portfolios with minimal human intervention. The robo-advisor has gained popularity among investors for its low fees and personalized approach.

AI in Financial Reporting

Understanding AI in Financial Reporting

Financial reporting is essential for businesses to communicate their financial performance to stakeholders. AI has the potential to transform financial reporting by automating the collection, analysis, and presentation of financial data. AI systems can extract information from various sources, including invoices, receipts, and bank statements, to generate accurate and timely financial reports.

These AI-driven systems can also identify discrepancies and anomalies in financial data, ensuring the integrity of financial reports. By automating routine reporting tasks, AI allows finance professionals to focus on more strategic activities, such as interpreting financial results and advising on business decisions.

Benefits of AI in Financial Reporting

The use of AI in financial reporting offers numerous benefits. It can significantly reduce the time and effort required to prepare financial statements, leading to cost savings and increased efficiency. AI also improves the accuracy of financial reports by minimizing human errors and inconsistencies.

Additionally, AI can provide real-time financial insights, enabling businesses to respond quickly to changing financial conditions. AI-driven financial reporting can also facilitate compliance with regulatory requirements by ensuring that financial statements are prepared in accordance with relevant accounting standards and regulations.

Case Studies of AI in Financial Reporting

A case study in this area involves a large corporation that implemented an AI system to automate its financial reporting process. The system streamlined the preparation of quarterly and annual financial statements, reducing the reporting cycle by several days. This allowed the company to release financial results to the market more quickly, providing a competitive advantage.

Another case study features a public accounting firm that used AI to analyze client financial data for audit purposes. The AI system was able to identify potential areas of risk and focus the audit efforts on those areas, improving the quality and efficiency of the audit process.

Future of AI in Financial Management

Emerging AI Technologies in Financial Management

The future of AI in financial management is promising, with new technologies emerging that have the potential to further transform the field. One such technology is blockchain, which, when combined with AI, can enhance the security and transparency of financial transactions. Another emerging technology is quantum computing, which could enable even faster and more complex financial data analysis.

Additionally, advancements in natural language processing (NLP) are making it possible for AI systems to understand and interpret financial news and reports, providing deeper insights into market conditions. The integration of AI with the Internet of Things (IoT) is also expected to provide new sources of financial data that can be used to inform financial management decisions.

Ethical Considerations in AI Financial Management

As AI technologies become more prevalent in financial management, ethical considerations must be addressed. Issues such as data privacy, algorithmic bias, and the potential for AI to replace human jobs are of concern. Ensuring that AI systems are transparent, fair, and accountable is essential to maintaining trust in financial management processes.

Businesses must also consider the implications of AI on financial inclusion, ensuring that AI-driven financial services are accessible to all segments of society. Additionally, the potential for AI to be used for malicious purposes, such as financial fraud or market manipulation, must be mitigated through robust security measures and ethical guidelines.

AI in Financial Management: Opportunities and Challenges

The opportunities presented by AI in financial management are vast, including increased efficiency, accuracy, and the ability to make data-driven decisions. However, there are also challenges to be overcome, such as the need for skilled professionals who can manage and interpret AI systems, the integration of AI with existing financial processes, and regulatory compliance.

As AI continues to evolve, businesses will need to stay informed about the latest developments and be prepared to adapt their financial management practices accordingly. By embracing AI and addressing the associated challenges, businesses can leverage the full potential of AI to enhance their financial management and gain a competitive edge in the marketplace.

Review Questions

1. What is one of the benefits of using AI in Financial Planning?
2. How does AI contribute to Risk Management in finance?
3. What role does AI play in Fraud Detection in finance?
4. How does AI assist in Investment Management?
5. What is one of the future challenges of AI in Financial Management?
6. What are some benefits of using AI in financial planning?
7. How does AI contribute to risk management in finance?
8. What are some ethical considerations when using AI in financial management?

CHAPTER 7

AI in Operations and Logistics

AI in Supply Chain Management

Artificial Intelligence (AI) in supply chain management refers to the use of machine learning algorithms, predictive analytics, and other AI technologies to optimize the flow of goods from suppliers to customers. AI systems can analyze vast amounts of data to forecast demand, identify supply chain risks, and suggest actions to improve efficiency and reduce costs. By integrating AI into supply chain operations, businesses can gain real-time insights into their logistics networks, enabling proactive decision-making and enhanced operational agility.

AI technologies such as natural language processing (NLP) and computer vision are also employed to automate routine tasks like document processing and quality inspections. This not only speeds up operations but also minimizes human error. Furthermore, AI-driven supply chain management can adapt to changing conditions, such as fluctuations in customer demand or disruptions in supply, ensuring that the supply chain remains resilient and responsive.

Benefits of AI in Supply Chain Management

The benefits of incorporating AI into supply chain management are multifaceted. One of the primary advantages is the enhancement of demand forecasting. AI algorithms can predict future product demand with high accuracy by analyzing historical sales data, market trends, and consumer behavior patterns. This allows companies to optimize inventory levels, reducing both overstock and stockouts, and thus saving on storage costs and improving customer satisfaction.

AI also improves supply chain visibility and traceability. By leveraging IoT devices and AI, companies can track products throughout the supply chain in real-time. This transparency helps in quickly identifying and addressing bottlenecks, reducing the risk of delays, and ensuring compliance with regulatory standards. Additionally, AI can assist in supplier selection and management by evaluating supplier performance data to recommend the most reliable and cost-effective partners.

Case Studies of AI in Supply Chain Management

A notable case study involves a global retail company that implemented AI to optimize its supply chain. The company used machine learning to analyze customer purchasing patterns and seasonal trends, which allowed it to adjust its inventory in real-time, leading to a 20% reduction in inventory costs and a significant improvement in customer satisfaction due to better product availability.

Another case study features a manufacturing firm that employed AI to enhance its supplier risk management. By using

AI to monitor and analyze news, social media, and weather forecasts, the company could predict and mitigate risks such as supplier bankruptcies or natural disasters. This proactive approach resulted in a more resilient supply chain and a reduction in unplanned downtime.

Further Reading

If you're interested in learning more about how AI is revolutionizing operations and logistics, visit www.christopherdessi.com/resources

AI in Inventory Management

Understanding AI in Inventory Management

AI in inventory management involves the application of machine learning models to predict optimal stock levels, automate reordering processes, and manage warehouse space efficiently. By analyzing sales data, customer demand patterns, and external factors such as holidays or economic indicators, AI systems can provide accurate inventory forecasts. These forecasts enable businesses to maintain the right amount of stock to meet customer demand without incurring excess holding costs.

Additionally, AI can categorize inventory based on various factors such as sales velocity, seasonality, and profitability. This categorization helps businesses prioritize their focus on high-impact items and optimize their inventory turnover rates. AI-driven inventory management systems can also suggest dynamic pricing strategies to clear excess stock and maximize revenue.

Benefits of AI in Inventory Management

The implementation of AI in inventory management brings several benefits, including reduced operational costs due to optimized stock levels. By preventing overstocking and understocking, companies can minimize capital tied up in inventory and reduce the risk of obsolescence. AI also enhances the responsiveness of inventory systems, allowing businesses to adapt quickly to changes in demand or supply chain disruptions.

Another significant benefit is the automation of inventory-related tasks. AI systems can automate order processing, stock replenishment, and even negotiate with suppliers for just-in-time deliveries. This automation not only saves time but also reduces the likelihood of human error, leading to more accurate inventory records and improved decision-making.

Case Studies of AI in Inventory Management

A leading electronics retailer leveraged AI to manage its inventory across hundreds of stores. By using predictive analytics, the retailer could anticipate product demand at each location and adjust inventory levels accordingly. This resulted in a 30% decrease in stockouts and a 25% reduction in excess inventory, translating to millions of dollars in savings.

In another instance, a pharmaceutical company implemented AI to manage its complex inventory of medications with varying shelf lives. The AI system provided insights into optimal stock levels and expiration date management, ensuring that the company could meet patient needs without wasting medication. This led to a significant reduction in waste and improved patient outcomes.

AI in Warehouse Management

Understanding AI in Warehouse Management

AI in warehouse management encompasses the use of machine learning, robotics, and automation technologies to streamline warehouse operations. AI systems can optimize the layout of warehouses, direct autonomous robots for picking and packing, and manage the flow of goods in and out of the facility. By analyzing historical data and real-time inputs, AI can continuously improve warehouse processes, such as the routing of robots or the placement of goods to minimize travel time and improve efficiency.

AI-driven warehouse management systems (WMS) can also predict future inventory needs and suggest optimal replenishment schedules. These systems integrate with other supply chain components to provide a cohesive view of operations, enabling better coordination and planning.

Benefits of AI in Warehouse Management

The benefits of AI in warehouse management are significant. AI enables warehouses to operate with greater precision and speed, leading to faster order fulfillment and improved customer satisfaction. By optimizing storage space and reducing unnecessary movement, AI can also lower energy consumption and operational costs.

Furthermore, AI enhances worker safety by automating dangerous or repetitive tasks, reducing the risk of injuries. It also allows for better workforce management by predicting peak periods and suggesting optimal staffing levels. This dynamic approach to workforce planning ensures that warehouses can handle fluctuations in demand without overstaffing or understaffing.

Case Studies of AI in Warehouse Management

A prominent e-commerce company implemented AI in its warehouses to manage a vast inventory and fulfill orders rapidly. The company used AI-powered robots to retrieve items, which doubled the speed of order processing and reduced human error. The AI system also optimized the warehouse layout, leading to a 20% increase in storage capacity without expanding the physical space.

Another case study involves a food distribution company that used AI to improve the freshness of its products. The AI system tracked expiration dates and prioritized the shipment of products close to their sell-by date. This not only reduced food waste but also ensured that customers received the freshest products possible.

AI in Transportation and Delivery

Understanding AI in Transportation and Delivery

AI in transportation and delivery involves the use of algorithms to optimize routing, manage fleets, and predict delivery times. By analyzing traffic patterns, weather conditions, and delivery histories, AI can determine the most efficient routes, reducing fuel consumption and delivery times. AI can also predict maintenance needs for vehicles, preventing breakdowns and extending the lifespan of the fleet.

In addition to route optimization, AI technologies such as autonomous vehicles and drones are beginning to transform delivery methods. These technologies promise to reduce the need for human drivers, increase delivery speed, and access hard-to-reach areas.

Benefits of AI in Transportation and Delivery

The integration of AI in transportation and delivery offers numerous benefits, including cost savings from reduced fuel consumption and improved fleet management. AI's predictive capabilities also enhance customer service by providing accurate delivery estimates and real-time tracking information.

Moreover, AI can improve sustainability by optimizing routes to minimize emissions and by facilitating the adoption of electric and autonomous vehicles. As transportation and delivery networks become more complex, AI's ability to manage and optimize these networks becomes increasingly valuable.

Case Studies of AI in Transportation and Delivery

A logistics company utilized AI to optimize its delivery routes, resulting in a 15% reduction in delivery times and a 10% decrease in fuel costs. The AI system also helped the company to dynamically adjust routes in response to traffic or weather disruptions, ensuring timely deliveries.

Another example is a food delivery service that used AI to predict delivery times more accurately. By analyzing historical data and real-time traffic information, the AI system provided customers with precise delivery windows, which improved customer satisfaction and reduced the number of customer service inquiries.

AI in Quality Control

Understanding AI in Quality Control

AI in quality control refers to the application of machine learning and computer vision to detect defects, ensure product consistency, and maintain high standards of quality. AI systems can analyze images and sensor data to identify anomalies in products or processes that may indicate quality issues. This allows for real-time monitoring and immediate corrective action, reducing the likelihood of defective products reaching customers.

AI can also predict potential quality issues before they occur by analyzing patterns in production data. This predictive quality control helps companies to address root causes and prevent defects, leading to a more reliable manufacturing process.

Benefits of AI in Quality Control

The benefits of AI in quality control are substantial. AI enables higher accuracy in defect detection compared to manual inspections, leading to fewer recalls and enhanced brand reputation. By automating quality inspections, AI also frees up human workers to focus on more complex tasks that require human judgment.

Additionally, AI-driven quality control systems can operate continuously, providing 24/7 monitoring without the need for breaks or shift changes. This constant vigilance ensures that quality issues are identified and addressed promptly, minimizing waste and improving overall production efficiency.

Case Studies of AI in Quality Control

An automotive manufacturer implemented AI in its quality control processes, using computer vision to inspect car parts for defects. The AI system achieved a 99% accuracy rate in defect detection, significantly higher than the previous manual inspection process. This led to a reduction in customer complaints and a stronger market position for the manufacturer.

In the textile industry, a company used AI to monitor fabric quality during production. The AI system identified variations in color and texture that were imperceptible to the human eye, ensuring that only the highest quality fabric was used in the final products. This attention to detail resulted in a premium product line that commanded higher prices and increased customer loyalty.

Did You Know?

AI is not just for big industries! While the examples provided highlight the use of AI in automotive and textile industries, it's important to know that AI can be used in a wide range of businesses, big or small.

AI in Small Businesses

Even small businesses can leverage AI to improve their operations. For example, a small bakery could use AI to predict the number of pastries they should bake each day based on historical sales data and weather forecasts. This could help reduce waste and increase profits.

AI in Service Industries

Service industries like hospitality and healthcare are also starting to use AI. Hotels are using AI to personalize guest experiences, while hospitals are using AI to predict patient health outcomes and optimize treatment plans.

AI in Agriculture

AI is even being used in agriculture to predict crop yields, optimize irrigation, and detect plant diseases. These applications of AI can help farmers increase their productivity and reduce their environmental impact.

AI in Education

AI is also making its way into the education sector. AI-powered tutoring systems can provide personalized learning experiences for students, while AI-driven administrative tools can help schools manage their resources more efficiently.

Future of AI in Operations and Logistics

Emerging AI Technologies in Operations and Logistics

The future of AI in operations and logistics is poised for significant advancements with emerging technologies such as blockchain for enhanced traceability, Internet of Things (IoT) for interconnected devices, and advanced robotics for autonomous operations. These technologies will further integrate AI into the supply chain, creating a more cohesive and intelligent logistics ecosystem.

Blockchain, when combined with AI, can provide a secure and transparent ledger for all transactions within the supply chain, ensuring data integrity and facilitating trust among stakeholders. IoT devices equipped with AI can monitor the condition of goods in real-time, enabling predictive maintenance and improving the overall quality of products. Advanced robotics, powered by AI, will continue to evolve, taking on more complex tasks and operating with greater autonomy in warehouses and manufacturing environments.

Ethical Considerations in AI Operations and Logistics

As AI technologies become more prevalent in operations and logistics, ethical considerations must be addressed. Issues such as job displacement, data privacy, and algorithmic bias need careful consideration. Companies must ensure that the transition to AI-enhanced operations includes retraining programs for employees and transparent data practices that respect customer privacy.

Algorithmic bias can also affect decision-making in supply chain management, potentially leading to unfair practices or discrimination. It is crucial for businesses to audit their AI systems regularly to identify and mitigate any biases that may arise.

AI in Operations and Logistics: Opportunities and Challenges

The opportunities presented by AI in operations and logistics are vast, offering the potential for significant efficiency gains, cost reductions, and service improvements. However, challenges such as integration with legacy systems, the need for skilled personnel to manage AI technologies, and the potential for cyber threats must be navigated.

To capitalize on the opportunities and overcome the

challenges, businesses must adopt a strategic approach to AI implementation, focusing on continuous learning and adaptation. Collaboration between industry players, technology providers, and regulatory bodies will also be essential to ensure that AI is used responsibly and effectively in operations and logistics.

In conclusion, AI is transforming operations and logistics, offering innovative solutions to traditional challenges and paving the way for a more efficient and responsive supply chain. As businesses continue to adopt AI, they will be better positioned to meet the demands of an increasingly complex and dynamic global market.

Review Questions

1. What is one of the benefits of AI in Supply Chain Management?

2. How does AI contribute to Inventory Management?

3. What is a key benefit of AI in Warehouse Management?

4. How does AI contribute to Quality Control in operations and logistics?
5. What is one of the future challenges for AI in Operations and Logistics?
6. What are some benefits of using AI in Supply Chain Management?
7. How can AI be utilized in Inventory Management?
8. What are some potential future applications of AI in Operations and Logistics?

CHAPTER 8

AI in Human Resources

AI in Recruitment and Hiring

The integration of Artificial Intelligence (AI) in recruitment and hiring processes is transforming how companies identify, attract, and hire talent. AI in recruitment encompasses a range of technologies, including machine learning algorithms, natural language processing, and predictive analytics, which can streamline the hiring process and enhance decision-making. These technologies can analyze large volumes of data to identify patterns and insights that human recruiters might overlook, such as subtle correlations between candidate attributes and job performance.

AI-powered tools can automate repetitive tasks such as resume screening, candidate sourcing, and initial candidate communications. This not only saves time but also helps reduce unconscious bias by ensuring that initial screening is based on data-driven criteria rather than human assumptions. Additionally, AI can enhance candidate engagement through chatbots that provide timely responses and personalized interactions, improving the overall candidate experience.

Benefits of AI in Recruitment and Hiring

The benefits of AI in recruitment and hiring are manifold. One of the primary advantages is the significant time savings for HR professionals. By automating the initial stages of the hiring process, such as resume screening and scheduling interviews, AI allows recruiters to focus on more strategic tasks. Furthermore, AI can increase the quality of hires by using predictive models to assess which candidates are most likely to succeed in a role.

Another benefit is the reduction of bias in the hiring process. AI algorithms can be designed to ignore demographic information such as age, gender, and ethnicity, focusing solely on skills and qualifications. This leads to a more diverse and inclusive workforce. Additionally, AI can improve the candidate experience by providing instant feedback and updates, maintaining engagement throughout the recruitment process.

Case Studies of AI in Recruitment and Hiring

Several companies have successfully implemented AI in their recruitment processes. For instance, a multinational technology company used an AI-powered tool to analyze job descriptions and candidate profiles, resulting in a 20% increase in the number of qualified candidates reaching the interview stage. Another case study involves a retail giant that implemented an AI chatbot for initial candidate interactions, which led to a 50% reduction in the time to hire and a significant improvement in candidate satisfaction scores.

These case studies demonstrate the potential of AI to revolutionize recruitment and hiring by making it more efficient, equitable, and candidate-friendly. As AI technology continues to evolve, it is likely that its role in recruitment will become even more prominent, with new tools and applications emerging to address the ever-changing needs of the job market.

AI in Employee Onboarding

Understanding AI in Employee Onboarding

Employee onboarding is a critical phase in the employee lifecycle, setting the tone for a new hire's experience with the company. AI in employee onboarding can personalize the process, making it more engaging and efficient. AI systems can guide new employees through paperwork, training modules, and company policies, adapting the pace and content to the individual's learning style and progress.

Moreover, AI can facilitate the integration of new hires into the company culture by connecting them with mentors and peers, recommending internal networks, and suggesting events that align with their interests and job roles. This personalized approach helps new employees feel welcomed and valued from day one, increasing their engagement and retention.

Benefits of AI in Employee Onboarding

The use of AI in employee onboarding offers several benefits, including consistency in delivering information, which ensures that all new hires receive the same level of training and support. It also provides scalability, allowing companies to onboard multiple employees simultaneously without compromising the quality of the experience.

AI-driven onboarding can also provide actionable insights to HR teams by analyzing new hire feedback and performance during the onboarding process. These insights can be used to continuously improve the onboarding experience and identify areas where additional support may be needed.

Case Studies of AI in Employee Onboarding

A leading financial services firm implemented an AI-driven onboarding platform that personalized the onboarding journey for each new hire. The platform provided tailored learning paths, automated document processing, and introduced gamification elements to make the process more engaging. As a result, the firm saw a 30% increase in new hire productivity within the first three months.

Another case study involves a healthcare provider that used AI to match new nurses with experienced mentors based on personality and professional interests. This led to a more effective mentorship program and a 25% decrease in turnover rates among new nurses in the first year.

Test Your Knowledge

Let's see how well you understood the case studies of AI in employee onboarding!

1. What kind of firm implemented an AI-driven onboarding platform that personalized the onboarding journey for each new hire?
2. What were the key features of the AI-driven onboarding platform used by the financial services firm?
3. What was the impact of implementing the AI-driven onboarding platform on new hire productivity?
4. Which sector used AI to match new nurses with experienced mentors?
5. What were the criteria used by the AI system to match new nurses with mentors?
6. What was the impact of using AI in the mentorship program on turnover rates among new nurses?

AI in Performance Management

Understanding AI in Performance Management

Performance management is evolving from an annual review process to a continuous, data-driven approach, thanks in part to AI. AI in performance management involves the use of machine learning algorithms to analyze employee data, providing real-time feedback and identifying development opportunities. AI can track progress on goals, monitor engagement levels, and even predict future performance based on current trends.

By leveraging AI, companies can move away from subjective assessments and towards a more objective, transparent, and personalized performance management system. This not only helps employees understand how they can improve but also fosters a culture of continuous learning and growth.

Benefits of AI in Performance Management

AI-driven performance management systems offer several benefits, including the ability to provide timely and specific feedback to employees, which can lead to immediate improvements in performance. These systems can also identify high performers and potential leaders within the organization, aiding succession planning and talent development.

Additionally, AI can help mitigate bias in performance evaluations by focusing on measurable outcomes and behaviors rather than subjective opinions. This leads to fairer assessments and can help build trust in the performance management process.

Case Studies of AI in Performance Management

A global consulting firm implemented an AI system that analyzed project outcomes, client feedback, and peer reviews to provide comprehensive performance insights for its consultants. This approach led to a more nuanced understanding of individual contributions and a 15% increase in overall team performance.

In another example, a technology startup used an AI platform to track employee engagement and performance metrics, which allowed managers to provide personalized coaching and support. The platform's predictive capabilities also helped the company anticipate and address potential performance issues before they became problematic.

Famous Quotes

"The future of business is in AI." - Andrew Ng, Co-founder of Coursera and Adjunct Professor at Stanford University

"Artificial Intelligence, deep learning, machine learning — whatever you're doing if you don't understand it — learn it. Because otherwise you're going to be a dinosaur within 3 years." - Mark Cuban, Entrepreneur and Investor

AI in Employee Engagement

Understanding AI in Employee Engagement

Employee engagement is a key driver of organizational success, and AI is playing an increasingly important role in measuring and enhancing it. AI tools can analyze employee feedback from surveys, emails, and other communication channels to gauge sentiment and engagement levels. These insights can then inform targeted interventions to improve the workplace experience.

AI can also personalize employee experiences by recommending learning opportunities, career paths, and even wellness programs based on individual preferences and performance data. This level of personalization helps employees feel valued and understood, which can significantly boost engagement.

Benefits of AI in Employee Engagement

The benefits of using AI in employee engagement are numerous. AI can provide a more accurate and comprehensive picture of engagement across the organization, identifying both strengths and areas for improvement. It can also deliver personalized experiences at scale, something that would be impossible for HR teams to do manually for every employee.

Furthermore, AI-driven engagement strategies can lead to higher retention rates, as employees are more likely to stay with a company that invests in their development and well-being. This, in turn, can lead to cost savings related to turnover and recruitment.

Case Studies of AI in Employee Engagement

A leading e-commerce company used an AI platform to analyze employee feedback and identify key drivers of engagement within their workforce. The insights gained allowed the company to implement targeted initiatives that resulted in a 40% improvement in employee satisfaction scores.

Another case study comes from a manufacturing firm that introduced an AI-powered wellness program. The program provided personalized health recommendations and challenges based on individual health data and preferences. Participation in the program led to a noticeable increase in overall employee well-being and a reduction in sick days.

AI in Training and Development

Understanding AI in Training and Development

Training and development are essential for keeping employees skilled and motivated. AI is transforming this area by offering personalized learning experiences that adapt to the learner's pace, preferences, and performance. AI-powered learning management systems (LMS) can curate content, assess skills gaps, and even predict which skills will be most valuable in the future.

These systems can also facilitate microlearning, delivering short, focused training modules that are easier to digest and apply. Additionally, AI can create realistic simulations and virtual environments for hands-on learning experiences that are both engaging and effective.

Benefits of AI in Training and Development

AI in training and development offers numerous benefits, including increased efficiency in learning by providing content that is directly relevant to the learner's needs. It also supports better retention of information through adaptive learning techniques that reinforce knowledge at optimal intervals.

Moreover, AI can help organizations identify future skill needs and prepare their workforce accordingly, ensuring that employees remain competitive and the company stays ahead of industry trends. This proactive approach to skill development can be a significant competitive advantage.

Case Studies of AI in Training and Development

A prominent software company implemented an AI-driven LMS that personalized learning paths for each developer based on their expertise and project requirements. This approach reduced the time needed to acquire new skills by 25% and increased the relevance of training content, leading to more innovative product development.

In the healthcare sector, a hospital used AI to create virtual reality simulations for surgical training. These simulations allowed surgeons to practice complex procedures in a risk-free environment, improving their skills and confidence. The program was credited with a significant reduction in surgical errors and improved patient outcomes.

Future of AI in Human Resources

Emerging AI Technologies in Human Resources

The future of AI in human resources is bright, with emerging technologies poised to further transform the field. For example, augmented reality (AR) and virtual reality (VR) are being explored for immersive training experiences. Blockchain technology is being considered for secure and transparent employee credential verification. Additionally, advanced analytics and big data are expected to provide even deeper insights into workforce trends and behaviors.

These technologies have the potential to create more efficient, personalized, and engaging HR processes, from recruitment to retirement. As AI becomes more sophisticated, it will continue to augment human capabilities in HR, enabling professionals to focus on strategic initiatives and human interactions that require empathy and nuanced judgment.

Ethical Considerations in AI Human Resources

As AI becomes more prevalent in HR, ethical considerations must be addressed. Issues such as data privacy, consent, and security are paramount, as HR departments handle sensitive personal information. There is also the risk of bias in AI algorithms, which must be carefully monitored and mitigated to ensure fair treatment of all employees.

Transparency in AI decision-making processes is another ethical concern. Employees should understand how AI is being used in HR processes and how it impacts them. This transparency builds trust and acceptance of AI tools within the organization.

AI in Human Resources: Opportunities and Challenges

The opportunities presented by AI in HR are vast, including the potential for enhanced employee experiences, more efficient HR operations, and better decision-making. However, challenges such as ensuring the accuracy of AI predictions, integrating AI with existing HR systems, and managing the change within organizations must be overcome.

To fully realize the benefits of AI in HR, companies must invest in the right technologies, develop clear strategies for implementation, and provide training for HR professionals and employees. With careful planning and ethical considerations, AI can significantly contribute to the success of human resources and, by extension, the entire organization.

Review Questions

1. How can AI be beneficial in the recruitment and hiring process?
2. What is a potential benefit of AI in employee onboarding?
3. How can AI be used in performance management?
4. What is a potential benefit of AI in employee engagement?
5. How can AI be used in training and development?
6. What are some benefits of using AI in recruitment and hiring?
7. How can AI be used in employee onboarding?
8. What are some ethical considerations when using AI in human resources?

CHAPTER 9

AI in Product Development

AI in Product Design

Artificial Intelligence (AI) in product design is revolutionizing the way products are conceived and brought to life. AI algorithms can analyze vast amounts of data, recognize patterns, and suggest design modifications that optimize for various factors, including functionality, aesthetics, and cost-efficiency. Tools powered by AI can simulate how a product will perform under different conditions, enabling designers to make informed decisions early in the design process.

The integration of AI into product design also facilitates generative design, where AI proposes design options based on specific parameters set by the designer. This approach not only speeds up the design process but also uncovers innovative solutions that may not have been considered by human designers.

Benefits of AI in Product Design

The benefits of AI in product design are manifold. AI-driven design tools can significantly reduce the time it takes to develop a product by automating repetitive tasks and generating multiple design iterations quickly. This acceleration allows companies to bring products to market faster, giving them a competitive edge.

AI also enhances the quality of product design by enabling precision and the ability to predict how design choices will impact the final product. By analyzing historical data, AI can help designers avoid past mistakes and replicate successes. Moreover, AI can optimize designs for sustainability, ensuring products are more eco-friendly and resource-efficient.

Case Studies of AI in Product Design

One notable case study involves a leading automotive company that used AI to redesign critical engine components. The AI system suggested a design that reduced the component's weight by 20% without compromising strength, resulting in better fuel efficiency and reduced emissions.

Another example is a furniture manufacturer that implemented AI to create ergonomic designs. The AI analyzed customer feedback and ergonomic data to design furniture that not only looked appealing but also provided improved comfort and support.

Quick Facts & Statistics

AI in Product Design

Did you know?

AI in Business

Interesting Statistics:

AI in Prototyping

Understanding AI in Prototyping

Prototyping is a crucial phase in product development where ideas are transformed into tangible models. AI accelerates this process by enabling rapid virtual prototyping. AI systems can create and test digital prototypes in virtual environments, simulating real-world conditions to predict performance and identify potential issues.

AI can also assist in physical prototyping by optimizing the use of materials and suggesting the most efficient manufacturing techniques. This not only saves time and resources but also allows for more iterations and improvements to be made in the prototyping stage.

Benefits of AI in Prototyping

AI-driven prototyping offers several benefits, including cost reduction by minimizing the need for physical prototypes. Virtual prototyping allows for extensive testing without the expense of creating multiple physical models. Additionally, AI can quickly adapt prototypes based on feedback, leading to a more iterative and responsive design process.

The use of AI in prototyping also enhances innovation by allowing designers to explore a wider range of possibilities.

AI can suggest novel materials and structures that might not be immediately apparent to human designers, leading to breakthroughs in product functionality and design.

Case Studies of AI in Prototyping

A tech company used AI to prototype a new wearable device. The AI analyzed user data to determine the most comfortable and practical design, which led to a prototype that received overwhelmingly positive feedback for its ergonomic design and ease of use.

In another instance, a sports equipment manufacturer employed AI to prototype a new type of running shoe. The AI simulated millions of running scenarios to create a shoe with optimal cushioning and support, which was then validated through physical prototyping.

AI in Product Testing

Understanding AI in Product Testing

Product testing is a critical step to ensure that a product is safe, reliable, and meets the intended quality standards. AI transforms product testing by automating the analysis of test results and identifying defects or areas for improvement. Machine learning models can predict failures before they occur by recognizing patterns in data collected from sensors and other sources.

AI can also simulate real-world usage scenarios to test products under a variety of conditions that would be difficult or impossible to replicate physically. This comprehensive testing ensures that products are robust and ready for the market.

Benefits of AI in Product Testing

The implementation of AI in product testing leads to higher quality products by enabling more thorough and precise testing. AI can uncover subtle issues that might be missed by traditional testing methods, reducing the risk of recalls or customer dissatisfaction.

AI also streamlines the testing process by automating routine tasks and analyzing data at a speed unattainable by human testers. This efficiency reduces the time and cost associated with bringing a product to market.

Case Studies of AI in Product Testing

A consumer electronics company used AI to test a new smartphone model. The AI performed stress tests and identified a potential overheating issue, which was then rectified before the product launch, averting a potential crisis.

Another case involved a medical device company that used AI to test a new diagnostic tool. The AI analyzed test results from clinical trials, speeding up the approval process and ensuring the device met all regulatory requirements.

AI in Product Launch

Understanding AI in Product Launch

A product launch is a critical moment for any business, and AI can play a significant role in ensuring its success. AI can analyze market trends, consumer behavior, and competitive landscapes to inform launch strategies. Predictive analytics can forecast demand, helping businesses to optimize inventory and supply chain management.

AI can also personalize marketing efforts, targeting potential customers with tailored messages and offers that are more likely to convert. By analyzing customer data, AI can identify the most effective channels and times to launch marketing campaigns, maximizing impact and reach.

Benefits of AI in Product Launch

Utilizing AI in product launches helps businesses to make data-driven decisions, reducing the risk of a failed launch. AI's predictive capabilities enable companies to align production with anticipated demand, preventing both shortages and excess inventory.

AI-driven marketing campaigns can increase the effectiveness of a product launch by ensuring that promotional efforts resonate with the target audience. This tailored approach can lead to higher engagement rates and a more successful market entry.

Case Studies of AI in Product Launch

A fashion retailer used AI to launch a new clothing line. The AI analyzed social media trends and past sales data to predict popular styles and sizes, resulting in a highly successful launch with record sales.

In the tech industry, a company launching a new app used AI to segment its audience and create personalized marketing campaigns. The AI's insights led to a launch strategy that achieved a high download rate and strong user retention.

Test Your Knowledge

Let's see how well you understood the role of AI in product launches. Try to answer the following questions:

1. How did the fashion retailer use AI to launch their new clothing line?

2. What kind of data did the AI analyze for the fashion retailer?
3. What was the result of using AI in the fashion retailer's product launch?
4. How did the tech company use AI in launching their new app?
5. What insights did the AI provide for the tech company's product launch?
6. What was the result of using AI in the tech company's product launch?

Review the case studies again if you're having trouble. Remember, understanding how AI can be leveraged in business is key to staying competitive in today's market!

AI in Post-Launch Analysis

Understanding AI in Post-Launch Analysis

After a product is launched, it's crucial to analyze its performance in the market. AI systems can continuously monitor sales data, customer reviews, and social media to gauge the product's reception. This real-time analysis provides valuable insights into customer satisfaction and areas for improvement.

AI can also track how a product is being used, identifying usage patterns that can inform future product updates or new product development. This ongoing analysis helps businesses stay responsive to customer needs and market changes.

Benefits of AI in Post-Launch Analysis

The benefits of AI in post-launch analysis include the ability to quickly identify and respond to issues, safeguarding the brand's reputation. AI can also uncover opportunities for product enhancements or identify successful features that can be replicated in future products.

By analyzing customer feedback, AI can provide actionable insights that lead to better customer experiences and increased loyalty. This continuous improvement cycle, driven by AI, can sustain a product's success in the market.

Case Studies of AI in Post-Launch Analysis

A video game company used AI to analyze player data and feedback after the launch of a new game. The insights gained allowed the company to release targeted updates that improved gameplay and increased player engagement.

Another example is a home appliance manufacturer that used AI to monitor the performance of a new kitchen gadget. The AI identified a feature that users found particularly useful, which the company then highlighted in subsequent marketing campaigns to boost sales.

Future of AI in Product Development

Emerging AI Technologies in Product Development

The future of AI in product development is poised for significant advancements with emerging technologies such as reinforcement learning, where AI systems learn optimal actions through trial and error. This could lead to even more autonomous design and testing processes.

Another promising area is the integration of AI with the Internet of Things (IoT), enabling smarter products that can adapt to user preferences and environmental changes. This convergence will likely result in products that are more responsive and personalized than ever before.

Ethical Considerations in AI Product Development

As AI becomes more integrated into product development, ethical considerations must be addressed. Issues such as data privacy, security, and the potential for AI to perpetuate biases must be carefully managed. Companies must ensure that AI systems are transparent and accountable, with safeguards in place to protect consumers and maintain trust.

AI in Product Development: Opportunities and Challenges

The opportunities presented by AI in product development are vast, offering the potential for more innovative, efficient, and customer-centric products. However, challenges such as ensuring data quality, managing complex AI systems, and keeping up with rapid technological changes must be overcome.

Companies that successfully navigate these challenges and harness the power of AI will be well-positioned to lead in their respective markets. The key to success will be a balanced approach that leverages AI's strengths while remaining vigilant about its limitations and ethical implications.

Review Questions

1. What is one of the benefits of using AI in product design?

2. How does AI contribute to the prototyping process?

3. What role does AI play in product testing?

4. How can AI assist in a product launch?

5. What is a key benefit of using AI in post-launch analysis?

6. What are some benefits of using AI in product design?
7. How can AI contribute to the prototyping phase of product development?
8. What are some ethical considerations to keep in mind when using AI in product development?

CHAPTER 10

AI in Sales and Revenue Generation

AI in Sales Forecasting

Sales forecasting is a critical component of business planning, allowing companies to make informed decisions about production, budgeting, and strategic planning. AI in sales forecasting involves the use of machine learning algorithms and predictive analytics to analyze historical sales data and identify patterns that can predict future sales. By leveraging large datasets, AI can uncover insights that would be difficult for humans to detect, such as subtle correlations between sales and external factors like economic indicators or social media trends.

The process begins with data collection, where AI systems gather sales figures, customer interactions, market trends, and other relevant data. This data is then cleaned and prepared for analysis. Machine learning models are trained on this data to recognize patterns and make predictions about future sales. These models can be continuously updated with new data to improve their accuracy over time.

Benefits of AI in Sales Forecasting

AI-driven sales forecasting offers numerous benefits over

traditional methods. One of the primary advantages is increased accuracy. AI models can process vast amounts of data and consider a wider range of variables, leading to more precise forecasts. This accuracy helps businesses reduce the risk of stockouts or overproduction, both of which can be costly.

Another benefit is the ability to perform real-time analysis. AI systems can quickly adjust forecasts based on the latest data, allowing businesses to respond swiftly to market changes. Additionally, AI can save time and resources by automating the data analysis process, freeing up sales teams to focus on strategy and customer engagement rather than number crunching.

Case Studies of AI in Sales Forecasting

Numerous companies have successfully implemented AI in their sales forecasting processes. For instance, a major retailer used AI to analyze transaction data across its stores, resulting in a 10% improvement in forecast accuracy. This led to better inventory management and a significant reduction in unsold stock.

Another case study involves a global beverage company that implemented AI to forecast sales for its thousands of products. The AI system considered factors such as weather patterns, promotional campaigns, and economic indicators. The result was a 5% increase in revenue due to more effective stock allocation and marketing strategies.

AI in Pricing Strategy

Understanding AI in Pricing Strategy

Pricing strategy is a complex task that involves setting the right price for products or services to maximize profits while remaining competitive. AI in pricing strategy uses machine learning to analyze data such as customer behavior, competitor pricing, and market conditions to determine optimal pricing. AI systems can also conduct price elasticity analysis to understand how changes in price affect demand.

Dynamic pricing is a common application of AI in pricing strategy. This approach allows businesses to adjust prices in real-time based on current market conditions. For example, online retailers can change the price of products throughout the day to respond to competitor pricing or changes in demand.

Benefits of AI in Pricing Strategy

AI enables businesses to adopt a data-driven approach to pricing, leading to several benefits. It allows for more granular pricing decisions at the product or customer segment level, which can increase profitability. AI can also identify opportunities for price optimization that humans might overlook, such as bundling products or offering targeted discounts.

Moreover, AI-driven pricing strategies can improve customer satisfaction by offering fair prices that reflect real-time market conditions. This can enhance brand loyalty and lead to increased sales over time.

Case Studies of AI in Pricing Strategy

One notable case study is an airline that used AI to optimize ticket pricing. The AI system analyzed data from past sales, competitor prices, and flight occupancy to adjust ticket prices dynamically. This resulted in a 7% increase in revenue per flight.

Another example is an e-commerce platform that implemented AI to personalize pricing for individual customers based on their purchase history and browsing behavior. This personalized approach led to a 15% increase in conversion rates and a significant boost in customer loyalty.

Further Reading

If you're intrigued by the potential of AI in pricing strategy and want to delve deeper into the subject, here are some recommended resources:

These resources provide a wealth of information on the practical applications of AI in pricing strategy. They offer valuable insights into how businesses can leverage AI to increase sales and revenue.

AI in Sales Automation

Understanding AI in Sales Automation

Sales automation involves using AI to streamline and enhance the sales process. AI can automate repetitive tasks such as data entry, lead qualification, and follow-up communications. It can also provide sales representatives with insights and recommendations, such as the best time to contact a lead or which products to recommend based on customer preferences.

AI-powered customer relationship management (CRM) systems are a key component of sales automation. These systems can analyze customer data to provide a 360-degree view of each customer, enabling personalized interactions and more effective sales strategies.

Benefits of AI in Sales Automation

The benefits of AI in sales automation are extensive. It can increase efficiency by reducing the time spent on administrative tasks, allowing sales teams to focus on building relationships and closing deals. AI can also improve the accuracy of lead scoring, ensuring that sales efforts are directed toward the most promising prospects.

Additionally, AI can enhance the customer experience by providing timely and relevant interactions, which can lead to higher conversion rates and increased customer loyalty.

Case Studies of AI in Sales Automation

A software company implemented an AI-powered CRM system that automated lead qualification and prioritization. This resulted in a 25% increase in sales productivity and a 20% increase in lead conversion rates.

Another case study involves a B2B services firm that used AI to automate its email marketing campaigns. The AI system analyzed customer interactions to determine the optimal timing and content for follow-up emails, leading to a 30% increase in engagement rates.

AI in Customer Retention

Understanding AI in Customer Retention

Customer retention is vital for long-term business success, and AI can play a significant role in retaining customers. AI systems can analyze customer behavior, purchase history, and feedback to identify signs of potential churn. By predicting which customers are at risk of leaving, businesses can proactively take steps to retain them, such as offering personalized incentives or addressing service issues.

AI can also help in segmenting customers based on their value and likelihood of churn, allowing businesses to tailor their retention strategies effectively.

Benefits of AI in Customer Retention

The use of AI in customer retention offers several benefits. It can improve the accuracy of churn predictions, enabling businesses to focus their retention efforts where they are most needed. AI can also help in creating a more personalized customer experience, which is a key factor in customer loyalty.

Furthermore, AI can identify patterns and triggers associated with churn, allowing businesses to address underlying issues and improve overall customer satisfaction.

Case Studies of AI in Customer Retention

A telecommunications company used AI to analyze call center data and social media feedback to predict customer churn. By identifying at-risk customers, the company was able to target them with retention campaigns, reducing churn by 15%.

In another example, an online streaming service used AI to personalize content recommendations based on viewing habits. This increased viewer engagement and reduced subscription cancellations by 20%.

Think & Reflect

Consider the power of AI in business:

Reflect on the potential of AI:

- How might AI change the way businesses operate in the future?
- What are some potential challenges businesses might face when implementing AI?
- How can businesses ensure they are using AI ethically and responsibly?

AI in Upselling and Cross-selling

Understanding AI in Upselling and Cross-selling

Upselling and cross-selling are sales techniques used to encourage customers to purchase higher-end products or additional items. AI can enhance these strategies by analyzing customer data to identify the most relevant products to recommend. By understanding a customer's preferences and purchase history, AI can make personalized recommendations that are more likely to result in a sale.

AI can also predict the best time to make these recommendations, such as when a customer is most engaged or when they have just made a purchase.

Benefits of AI in Upselling and Cross-selling

AI-driven upselling and cross-selling can lead to increased average order value and customer lifetime value. By making relevant recommendations, businesses can enhance the customer experience and build stronger relationships with their customers.

Additionally, AI can automate the recommendation process, making it scalable and efficient across large customer bases.

Case Studies of AI in Upselling and Cross-selling

A leading e-commerce platform used AI to recommend products based on items in a customer's shopping cart. This resulted in a 35% increase in average order value for customers who engaged with the recommendations.

Another case study comes from a financial services company that used AI to identify customers eligible for premium credit card offers. By targeting these customers with personalized offers, the company saw a 50% increase in upsell acceptance rates.

Future of AI in Sales and Revenue Generation

Emerging AI Technologies in Sales and Revenue Generation

The future of AI in sales and revenue generation is promising, with new technologies emerging that can further enhance sales processes. For example, conversational AI and voice recognition technologies are being developed to facilitate more natural interactions with customers, potentially increasing engagement and sales.

Augmented reality (AR) and virtual reality (VR) are also being explored for their potential to create immersive shopping experiences that can drive sales. Additionally, blockchain technology could be used to create more secure and transparent transactions, building trust with customers.

Ethical Considerations in AI Sales and Revenue Generation

As AI becomes more prevalent in sales and revenue generation, ethical considerations must be addressed. Issues such as data privacy, consent, and transparency are critical. Businesses must ensure that they use customer data responsibly and with permission, and that AI-driven decisions are fair and unbiased.

There is also a need for clear communication with customers about how their data is being used and how AI is influencing the sales process. This transparency can help maintain trust and prevent potential backlash.

AI in Sales and Revenue Generation:

Opportunities and Challenges

The opportunities presented by AI in sales and revenue generation are vast. AI can help businesses increase efficiency, improve customer experiences, and drive revenue growth. However, there are also challenges to be overcome, such as integrating AI with existing systems, ensuring data quality, and managing the change within organizations.

As AI continues to evolve, businesses will need to stay informed about the latest developments and be prepared to adapt their strategies to leverage AI effectively.

In conclusion, AI has the potential to transform sales and revenue generation, offering businesses new ways to engage with customers and drive growth. By understanding and embracing AI, businesses can position themselves for success in the competitive landscape of the future.

Review Questions

1. What is one of the benefits of using AI in sales

forecasting?

2. How does AI contribute to pricing strategy?
3. What is the role of AI in sales automation?
4. How does AI contribute to customer retention?
5. What is one of the benefits of using AI in upselling and cross-selling?
6. What are some benefits of using AI in sales forecasting?
7. How can AI be used in pricing strategy?
8. What are some ethical considerations when using AI in sales and revenue generation?

CHAPTER 11

AI and Business Analytics

AI in Data Collection

Data collection is a fundamental step in the business analytics process. It involves gathering information from various sources to be used for analysis. Artificial Intelligence (AI) enhances this process by automating data collection and enabling the extraction of data from complex and unstructured sources. AI systems can continuously collect data in real-time, ensuring that businesses have access to the most current information. This is particularly useful in environments where data is generated rapidly, such as social media platforms, sensors in the Internet of Things (IoT), and online transactions.

AI-driven data collection tools use techniques such as web scraping, natural language processing (NLP), and image recognition to gather data. These tools can identify patterns, trends, and anomalies that might be missed by human data collectors. By leveraging AI, businesses can collect a wider variety of data, including sentiment analysis from social media, consumer behavior patterns, and operational efficiency metrics.

Benefits of AI in Data Collection

The benefits of using AI in data collection are manifold. Firstly, AI increases the speed and efficiency of data collection, allowing businesses to process large volumes of data in a fraction of the time it would take manually. This speed means that businesses can react more quickly to market changes and consumer trends. Secondly, AI improves the accuracy of data collection by reducing human error and bias. AI algorithms can be trained to follow strict data collection protocols, ensuring consistency across data sets.

Another significant benefit is the ability of AI to collect and synthesize data from disparate sources, providing a more holistic view of the business landscape. This comprehensive data collection can lead to better-informed decision-making and strategy development. Additionally, AI can identify new data sources and types of data that can be valuable for businesses, leading to innovative approaches to market analysis and customer engagement.

Case Studies of AI in Data Collection

One notable case study involves a retail company that implemented AI to track customer behavior both online and in-store. By using AI-powered cameras and sensors, the company collected data on shopping patterns, product interactions, and even the expressions and emotions of shoppers. This data was then analyzed to optimize store layouts, product placements, and to personalize marketing efforts.

Another case study comes from the healthcare sector, where AI is used to collect patient data from various sources, including electronic health records, wearable devices, and genetic information. This comprehensive data collection allows for more accurate diagnoses, personalized treatment plans, and predictive health insights that can lead to preventative care measures.

Did You Know?

AI in Retail: AI is not just used for tracking customer behavior in stores. It's also used to manage inventory, predict trends, and even automate customer service through chatbots. Some retail companies are even using AI to create virtual fitting rooms, where customers can virtually try on clothes before making a purchase.

AI in Healthcare: Beyond data collection, AI is revolutionizing healthcare in many other ways. For example, AI algorithms are being used to read and interpret medical images, such as X-rays and MRIs, often with greater accuracy than human radiologists. AI is also being used to predict patient readmissions and to identify high-risk patients, which can help hospitals allocate resources more effectively.

AI Everywhere:

AI is not limited to retail and healthcare sectors. It's being used in a wide range of industries, including finance, agriculture, education, and transportation. In finance, AI is used for fraud detection and risk assessment. In agriculture, AI is used for crop and soil monitoring. In education, AI is used for personalized learning and grading automation. And in transportation, AI is used for route optimization and autonomous vehicles.

AI in Data Analysis

Understanding AI in Data Analysis

Data analysis is the process of examining, cleaning, transforming, and modeling data to discover useful information, inform conclusions, and support decision-making. AI transforms traditional data analysis by introducing advanced algorithms and machine learning techniques that can handle complex and voluminous data sets with ease. AI systems can detect patterns, correlations, and trends that are not immediately apparent to human analysts.

Machine learning, a subset of AI, is particularly influential in data analysis. It allows systems to learn from data, identify patterns, and make decisions with minimal human intervention. For example, unsupervised learning algorithms can cluster data into meaningful groups without prior labeling, while supervised learning algorithms can predict outcomes based on historical data.

Benefits of AI in Data Analysis

AI in data analysis offers several benefits, including the ability to process and analyze data at unprecedented speeds. This rapid analysis allows businesses to gain insights almost in real-time, which is crucial for time-sensitive decisions. AI also enables the analysis of unstructured data, such as text, images, and video, which constitutes a significant portion of the data businesses collect.

Furthermore, AI can provide more accurate predictions and models due to its ability to handle large and complex data sets. This accuracy leads to more reliable forecasting, which is essential for strategic planning and resource allocation. AI-driven data analysis can also uncover hidden insights that can lead to innovative products, services, and business models.

Case Studies of AI in Data Analysis

A financial institution used AI to analyze customer transaction data and identify patterns indicative of fraudulent activity. The AI system was able to flag suspicious transactions in real-time, allowing the bank to take immediate action to prevent fraud. This proactive approach not only protected customers but also saved the bank millions of dollars in potential losses.

In the field of e-commerce, an online retailer implemented AI algorithms to analyze customer reviews and feedback. The AI system categorized comments by sentiment and topic, providing the retailer with actionable insights into customer satisfaction and product performance. This analysis led to targeted improvements in product quality and customer service.

AI in Data Visualization

Understanding AI in Data Visualization

Data visualization is the graphical representation of information and data. By using visual elements like charts, graphs, and maps, data visualization tools provide an accessible way to see and understand trends, outliers, and patterns in data. AI enhances data visualization by automating the creation of visual representations and by offering advanced, interactive visualization techniques that can adapt to the user's needs.

AI-powered data visualization tools can analyze the underlying data and suggest the most effective types of visualizations for the specific insights being sought. They can also personalize dashboards and reports for individual users, highlighting the most relevant information based on their role or past interactions with the data.

Benefits of AI in Data Visualization

The integration of AI into data visualization brings several benefits. It allows for dynamic and real-time visualizations that can update as new data becomes available, providing a current snapshot of business metrics. AI can also handle complex, multi-dimensional data sets, creating visualizations that would be difficult or impossible for humans to generate manually.

Additionally, AI-driven data visualization can identify and highlight significant trends and patterns, directing users' attention to the most important insights. This feature is particularly useful in decision-making processes, where understanding the data quickly and accurately is crucial.

Case Studies of AI in Data Visualization

A logistics company used AI to visualize their global supply chain operations. The AI system provided interactive maps and graphs that displayed real-time shipping data, inventory levels, and potential bottlenecks. This visualization enabled the company to optimize routing, reduce delays, and manage inventory more effectively.

In another case, a city government employed AI to visualize traffic flow and congestion patterns. The AI system used data from traffic cameras, sensors, and GPS devices to create visualizations that helped city planners design better traffic management strategies and infrastructure improvements.

AI in Predictive Analytics

Understanding AI in Predictive Analytics

Predictive analytics is the use of data, statistical algorithms, and machine learning techniques to identify the likelihood of future outcomes based on historical data. AI plays a pivotal role in predictive analytics by providing the computational power and advanced modeling capabilities necessary to forecast future events with a high degree of accuracy.

AI systems can process vast amounts of historical data to train predictive models. These models can then be used to make predictions about future customer behavior, market trends, and operational risks. AI algorithms can continuously refine these models as more data becomes available, improving their accuracy over time.

Benefits of AI in Predictive Analytics

The use of AI in predictive analytics offers significant advantages. It enables businesses to anticipate market changes, customer needs, and potential risks, allowing them to take proactive measures. AI-driven predictions can lead to better resource allocation, targeted marketing campaigns, and improved product development strategies.

AI also democratizes predictive analytics by making it accessible to businesses of all sizes. Small and medium-sized enterprises can leverage cloud-based AI services to gain insights that were previously only available to large corporations with extensive data science teams.

Case Studies of AI in Predictive Analytics

A telecommunications company used AI to predict customer churn. By analyzing customer usage patterns, support interactions, and billing history, the AI model identified customers at risk of leaving. The company then implemented targeted retention strategies, which resulted in a significant reduction in churn rates.

In the energy sector, an AI system was used to predict demand and optimize electricity generation. The predictive model took into account weather patterns, historical consumption data, and economic indicators to forecast energy needs. This prediction allowed the utility company to adjust production, reducing waste and lowering costs.

Think & Reflect

Consider the power of AI in predictive analytics:

1. How did the telecommunications company benefit from using AI to predict customer churn? What strategies might they have implemented to retain customers identified as at risk?
2. Reflect on the use of AI in the energy sector. How did predictive analytics help the utility company optimize electricity generation and reduce waste?

3. Can you think of other industries where predictive analytics could be beneficial? How might AI be used in these contexts?

Remember: AI is not just about technology, it's about finding ways to make businesses more efficient and effective. As you read, think about how AI can be leveraged in different business scenarios for maximum benefit.

AI in Decision Making

Understanding AI in Decision Making

Decision making in business involves choosing between different courses of action to achieve desired outcomes. AI enhances decision-making processes by providing data-driven insights and recommendations. AI systems can analyze large data sets to identify the best options based on predefined criteria, such as cost, time, and potential return on investment.

AI can also simulate different scenarios to predict the outcomes of various decisions. This capability allows businesses to assess the potential impact of their choices before committing resources. Furthermore, AI can assist in real-time decision-making by processing new information as it becomes available and adjusting recommendations accordingly.

Benefits of AI in Decision Making

The integration of AI into decision-making processes offers numerous benefits. It leads to more informed and objective decisions by reducing the influence of human biases and emotions. AI can process a broader range of information than humans, considering factors that might be overlooked otherwise.

AI-driven decision-making can also increase efficiency by automating routine decisions, freeing up human managers to focus on more strategic tasks. Additionally, AI can improve the consistency of decision-making across an organization by ensuring that all decisions are based on the same data and criteria.

Case Studies of AI in Decision Making

A multinational corporation implemented an AI system to assist with investment decisions. The AI analyzed market data, financial reports, and industry trends to recommend the most promising investment opportunities. This approach resulted in higher returns and a more diversified portfolio.

In the healthcare industry, an AI-driven decision support system was used to assist doctors in diagnosing and treating patients. The system analyzed medical records, lab results, and clinical research to suggest the most effective treatments. This support led to better patient outcomes and more efficient use of healthcare resources.

Future of AI in Business Analytics

Emerging AI Technologies in Business Analytics

The future of AI in business analytics is marked by the continuous development of new technologies and techniques. Emerging AI technologies include advanced machine learning models like deep reinforcement learning, which can optimize complex decision-making processes. Quantum computing is another area that promises to revolutionize data analysis by performing calculations at speeds unattainable by traditional computers.

Another promising development is the integration of AI with blockchain technology, which can enhance data security and traceability in analytics. This combination could lead to more transparent and tamper-proof data analysis processes, increasing trust in AI-driven insights.

Ethical Considerations in AI Business Analytics

As AI becomes more prevalent in business analytics, ethical considerations must be addressed. Issues such as data privacy, bias in AI algorithms, and the potential for job displacement are of concern. Businesses must ensure that their use of AI in analytics complies with data protection laws and ethical standards.

Transparency in AI processes is also crucial. Stakeholders should understand how AI systems make decisions and on what basis. Efforts to develop explainable AI (XAI) are underway, aiming to make AI decision-making processes more understandable to humans.

AI in Business Analytics: Opportunities and Challenges

AI presents both opportunities and challenges in the field of business analytics. The opportunities include the potential for more accurate predictions, personalized customer experiences, and improved operational efficiency. AI can also help businesses to discover new markets and innovate in product and service offerings.

However, challenges such as ensuring data quality, managing the complexity of AI systems, and addressing the skills gap in AI expertise must be overcome. Businesses need to invest in training and development to build a workforce capable of working alongside AI. Additionally, they must navigate the evolving regulatory landscape around AI and data use.

In conclusion, AI is transforming the field of business analytics by enabling more efficient data collection, analysis, visualization, and decision-making. As technology advances, businesses must embrace AI to remain competitive while also considering the ethical implications of its use.

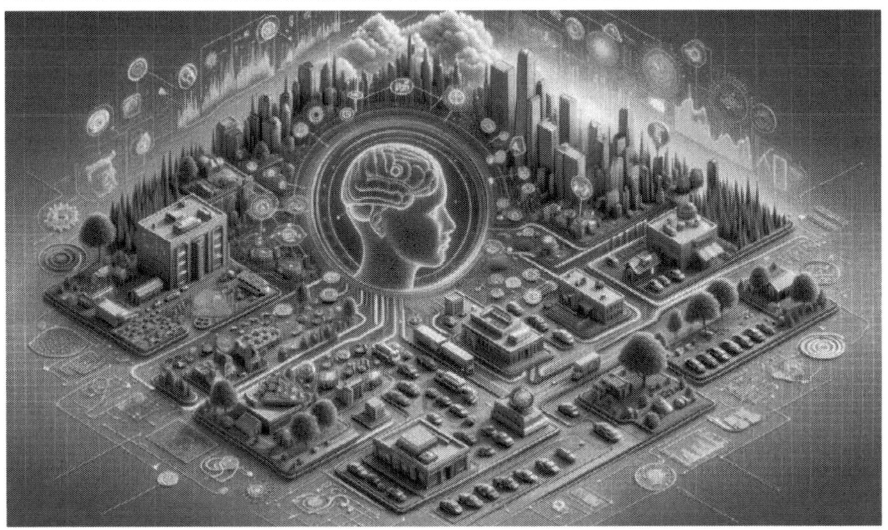

Review Questions

1. What is one of the benefits of AI in Data Collection?
2. How does AI in Data Analysis enhance business operations?
3. What is a key advantage of AI in Data Visualization?
4. What is the role of AI in Predictive Analytics?
5. What is a potential challenge for AI in Business

Analytics?

6. What are some benefits of using AI in data collection for business analytics?
7. How does AI contribute to predictive analytics in business?
8. What are some ethical considerations when using AI in business analytics?

CHAPTER 12

AI and Risk Management

AI in Risk Identification

Risk identification is the process of determining risks that could potentially prevent the program, enterprise, or investment from achieving its objectives. It includes documenting and communicating concerns about these risks with stakeholders and team members. In the context of AI, risk identification involves the use of advanced algorithms and machine learning techniques to predict and identify potential risks before they become critical issues. AI systems can process vast amounts of data to detect patterns and anomalies that may indicate a risk, which human analysts might overlook due to the sheer scale of the data.

AI-driven risk identification tools are capable of continuously monitoring various sources of data, including market trends, social media, internal performance metrics, and more. These tools can provide early warnings of potential financial, operational, compliance, or reputational risks. By leveraging natural language processing (NLP), AI can also scan through news articles, financial reports, and other textual data to identify risks that are not easily quantifiable.

Benefits of AI in Risk Identification

The benefits of using AI for risk identification are numerous. Firstly, AI can enhance the speed and accuracy of risk detection. Unlike traditional methods that rely on periodic reviews, AI systems can offer real-time risk assessment, allowing businesses to respond more quickly to potential threats. Secondly, AI can handle complex and high-volume datasets that are beyond human capacity to analyze, thus identifying subtle correlations and hidden patterns that might indicate emerging risks.

Another significant advantage is the predictive capability of AI. Machine learning models can forecast future risks based on historical data, enabling proactive risk management. This predictive power can be particularly beneficial in industries like finance or healthcare, where being able to anticipate risks can save substantial resources and even lives. Additionally, AI can democratize risk identification, making it accessible to smaller businesses that may not have the resources for extensive risk management teams.

Case Studies of AI in Risk Identification

One notable case study involves a global financial institution that implemented an AI system to monitor transactions for signs of fraudulent activity. The AI tool analyzed millions of transactions in real-time, identifying patterns consistent with fraud. This allowed the bank to freeze suspicious accounts and prevent significant financial losses.

Another example is a healthcare provider that used AI to identify risks in patient care. By analyzing electronic health records, the AI system could predict which patients were at risk of adverse events, such as hospital readmissions or complications. This enabled healthcare professionals to intervene earlier and improve patient outcomes.

AI in Risk Assessment

Understanding AI in Risk Assessment

Risk assessment involves evaluating the identified risks to understand their potential impact and the likelihood of their occurrence. AI enhances risk assessment by quantifying and prioritizing risks using advanced algorithms. AI systems can simulate various scenarios to predict the outcomes of different risk factors, helping organizations to focus their resources on the most significant threats.

AI models, especially those using machine learning, can be trained on historical data to understand the outcomes of past risk events. This training allows them to provide a more accurate assessment of current risks. AI can also combine data from disparate sources to give a more comprehensive view of risk, considering factors that may not be immediately apparent to human analysts.

Benefits of AI in Risk Assessment

AI systems can process and analyze data at a scale and speed that is impossible for humans, leading to more efficient and comprehensive risk assessments. They can also reduce the subjectivity in risk evaluation by consistently applying the same criteria to each risk scenario. This objectivity can be particularly valuable in regulatory compliance, where consistency in risk assessment is crucial.

Furthermore, AI can help in dynamic risk assessment, where the risk landscape is continuously changing. For example, in cybersecurity, threats evolve rapidly, and AI systems can adapt to these changes more quickly than traditional methods, providing up-to-date assessments that reflect the current threat environment.

Case Studies of AI in Risk Assessment

A tech company used AI to assess the risks associated with launching a new product in different markets. The AI analyzed market data, consumer trends, and competitive activity to provide a risk score for each market. This helped the company prioritize its market entry strategy and allocate resources effectively.

In the insurance industry, a company implemented AI to assess the risk of providing insurance to potential clients. By analyzing a wide range of factors, including driving records, credit scores, and even social media activity, the AI system could determine the likelihood of a claim being made and set premiums accordingly.

Did You Know?

AI is not just for big businesses! While the examples above show how large corporations use AI for risk assessment, small businesses can also benefit from AI technology. Here are a few ways:

So, no matter the size of your business, AI has something to offer!

AI in Risk Mitigation

Understanding AI in Risk Mitigation

Risk mitigation involves taking steps to reduce the potential impact of identified risks. AI contributes to risk mitigation by suggesting the most effective actions to minimize risk based on predictive models and historical data. AI systems can recommend a range of strategies, from simple corrective actions to complex plans involving multiple steps and stakeholders.

AI can also automate certain risk mitigation processes, such as patching software vulnerabilities or adjusting financial portfolios in response to market changes. This automation not only speeds up the response to risks but also ensures that mitigation strategies are implemented consistently across the organization.

Benefits of AI in Risk Mitigation

The use of AI in risk mitigation offers several benefits, including the ability to respond to risks in real-time. For example, AI systems can instantly reroute supply chains in response to a disruption, minimizing downtime and financial loss. AI can also scale risk mitigation efforts, applying them across different departments or geographic locations without the need for additional human resources.

Another benefit is the continuous improvement of mitigation strategies. As AI systems learn from each risk event, they can refine their recommendations, leading to more effective risk management over time. This learning capability is particularly important in fast-changing environments where new risks can emerge suddenly.

Case Studies of AI in Risk Mitigation

A multinational corporation used AI to mitigate the risk of

currency fluctuations impacting its profits. The AI system analyzed currency trends and recommended hedging strategies to protect against adverse movements. This proactive approach saved the company millions of dollars in potential losses.

Another case involved a retail chain that used AI to mitigate the risk of stockouts during peak shopping periods. The AI system forecasted demand for products at different locations and optimized inventory levels accordingly, ensuring that the stores could meet customer demand without overstocking.

AI in Crisis Management

Understanding AI in Crisis Management

Crisis management is the process of dealing with disruptive and unexpected events that threaten to harm an organization or its stakeholders. AI can play a crucial role in crisis management by providing rapid analysis of the situation and suggesting the most effective response. AI systems can monitor various indicators to detect early signs of a crisis, such as a sudden drop in brand sentiment on social media or unusual financial transactions that may indicate fraud.

During a crisis, AI can assist in coordinating response efforts, ensuring that all parts of the organization are working together effectively. AI can also simulate different response scenarios to predict their outcomes, helping decision-makers choose the best course of action.

Benefits of AI in Crisis Management

AI enhances crisis management by providing a rapid, data-driven response to unexpected events. It can process vast amounts of information from various sources to give a comprehensive view of the crisis, something that is often challenging to achieve in the heat of the moment. AI can also help maintain communication with stakeholders, automatically sending updates and instructions based on the evolving situation.

Another benefit is the ability of AI to learn from each crisis, improving the organization's response to future events. By analyzing the effectiveness of different strategies, AI can help organizations build more resilient crisis management plans.

Case Studies of AI in Crisis Management

A natural disaster provided an opportunity for a logistics company to leverage AI in crisis management. The AI system analyzed weather data and traffic patterns to reroute shipments away from the affected area, minimizing disruption to the supply chain and ensuring the safety of the delivery personnel.

In another instance, a social media platform used AI to manage a data breach crisis. The AI system identified the breach quickly and assessed its scope, allowing the company to secure affected accounts and communicate transparently with users about the steps being taken to resolve the issue.

Biographical Snapshot

Meet the Pioneers of AI in Business

Elon Musk: Known for his role in companies like Tesla and SpaceX, Musk has been a vocal advocate for the responsible use of AI. He co-founded OpenAI, a research organization dedicated to ensuring that artificial general intelligence (AGI) benefits all of humanity.

- Key Contribution: Co-founding OpenAI and promoting the ethical use of AI.

Andrew Ng: A co-founder of Google Brain and former chief scientist at Baidu, Ng is a leading figure in AI. He's also the co-founder of Coursera, an online learning platform that offers courses on AI and machine learning.

- Key Contribution: Advancing deep learning through Google Brain and promoting AI education through Coursera.

Fei-Fei Li: A computer science professor at Stanford University, Li is the co-director of Stanford's Human-Centered AI Institute. She's known for her work in developing ImageNet, a large visual database essential for recent developments in deep learning.

- Key Contribution: Developing ImageNet and advancing human-centered AI research.

AI in Compliance and Regulatory Risk

Understanding AI in Compliance and Regulatory Risk

Compliance and regulatory risk refer to the potential for legal penalties, financial forfeiture, and material loss an organization faces when it fails to act in accordance with industry laws and regulations. AI can assist organizations in navigating the complex landscape of compliance and regulatory requirements by monitoring changes in legislation and automatically adjusting compliance processes to stay up-to-date.

AI systems can also analyze internal data to ensure that all aspects of the business are compliant with relevant laws and regulations. This includes monitoring communications for potential breaches of conduct, tracking financial transactions for signs of money laundering, and ensuring that customer data is handled in accordance with privacy laws.

Benefits of AI in Compliance and Regulatory Risk

The use of AI in compliance and regulatory risk management offers several advantages. It can reduce the cost and complexity of compliance by automating routine tasks, such as report generation and data analysis. AI can also improve the accuracy of compliance efforts, reducing the risk of human error and ensuring that all regulatory requirements are met.

Additionally, AI can provide a more agile response to regulatory changes. As new laws are enacted or existing regulations are updated, AI systems can quickly adapt, ensuring that the organization remains compliant without the need for time-consuming manual processes.

Case Studies of AI in Compliance and Regulatory Risk

A financial services firm used AI to manage its compliance with anti-money laundering (AML) regulations. The AI system analyzed transaction data to identify patterns indicative of money laundering, flagging suspicious activity for further investigation by compliance officers.

Another case involved a healthcare provider that implemented AI to ensure compliance with patient privacy laws. The AI monitored access to patient records, detecting and alerting management to any unauthorized access or potential data breaches.

Future of AI in Risk Management

Emerging AI Technologies in Risk Management

The future of AI in risk management is promising, with new technologies emerging that will further enhance the ability of organizations to identify, assess, and mitigate risks. One such technology is the use of AI-powered predictive analytics, which can forecast potential risks with greater accuracy and provide recommendations for preemptive action.

Another emerging technology is the integration of AI with the Internet of Things (IoT). This combination allows for real-time monitoring of physical assets, providing immediate alerts when potential risks are detected. Blockchain technology is also being explored as a means to enhance transparency and security in risk management processes, particularly in financial transactions and supply chain operations.

Ethical Considerations in AI Risk Management

As AI becomes more integral to risk management, ethical considerations must be addressed. This includes ensuring that AI systems are transparent in their decision-making processes and that they do not perpetuate biases that could lead to unfair risk assessments. There is also a need to consider the privacy implications of using AI to monitor and analyze data, particularly when it involves sensitive personal information.

Organizations must establish clear guidelines and governance structures to manage these ethical concerns. This includes the development of ethical AI frameworks, regular audits of AI systems, and the inclusion of diverse perspectives in the design and implementation of AI solutions.

AI in Risk Management: Opportunities and Challenges

The opportunities presented by AI in risk management are vast. AI can transform how organizations approach risk, making it possible to manage complex, interconnected risks in a more efficient and effective manner. However, there are also challenges to be overcome, including the need for high-quality data to train AI systems, the potential for AI to introduce new risks, and the requirement for skilled personnel to manage and oversee AI-driven risk management processes.

To capitalize on the opportunities and address the challenges, organizations will need to invest in AI literacy and training, develop robust data management practices, and engage in cross-industry collaboration to share best practices and develop standards for AI in risk management.

Review Questions

1. Which of the following best describes the role of AI in risk identification?
2. What is a key benefit of using AI in risk assessment?
3. How does AI contribute to risk mitigation?
4. What role does AI play in crisis management?
5. What is a potential challenge for the future of AI in risk management?
6. What are some benefits of using AI in risk identification?
7. How does AI contribute to risk mitigation?
8. What are some ethical considerations in AI risk management?

CHAPTER 13

AI and Competitive Advantage

AI in Business Strategy

Artificial Intelligence (AI) has become a pivotal element in formulating business strategies. By integrating AI, companies can analyze vast amounts of data, predict trends, and make informed decisions. AI systems can identify patterns and insights that are beyond human capacity, enabling businesses to strategize with a level of precision and foresight previously unattainable. AI-driven strategy involves using algorithms and machine learning models to optimize operations, drive innovation, and enhance customer experiences.

The strategic application of AI can range from automating routine tasks to developing new products and services. It also includes leveraging AI for strategic decision-making, where predictive analytics can forecast market changes and consumer behavior. This allows companies to be proactive rather than reactive, adjusting their strategies to maintain a competitive edge.

Benefits of AI in Business Strategy

The benefits of incorporating AI into business strategy are manifold. AI enables real-time data analysis, which can lead to more agile and adaptive strategies. It also enhances efficiency by automating and optimizing processes, reducing costs, and increasing productivity. Furthermore, AI can improve decision-making by providing actionable insights and reducing the likelihood of human error.

Another significant benefit is the ability of AI to personalize customer experiences. By analyzing customer data, AI can help businesses tailor their offerings to individual preferences, increasing customer satisfaction and loyalty. Additionally, AI can uncover new market opportunities and niches by identifying trends and gaps in the market.

Case Studies of AI in Business Strategy

One notable case study is that of a global retailer that implemented AI to optimize its inventory management. By using machine learning algorithms to predict purchasing trends, the company was able to reduce stockouts and overstock, resulting in improved customer satisfaction and reduced costs.

Another example is a financial services firm that used AI to enhance its risk assessment models. By incorporating AI into their strategy, they were able to identify potential risks more accurately and take preemptive measures to mitigate them, thus protecting their assets and maintaining customer trust.

AI in Innovation and Productivity

Understanding AI in Innovation and Productivity

AI is a driving force behind innovation and productivity in businesses. It fosters the development of new products and services by analyzing market data and consumer feedback to identify unmet needs. AI can also streamline research and development processes, reducing the time and resources required to bring new ideas to market.

In terms of productivity, AI can automate repetitive and time-consuming tasks, freeing up human workers to focus on more complex and creative work. This not only increases output but also enhances job satisfaction among employees. AI can also optimize production lines in manufacturing, leading to fewer errors and higher quality products.

Benefits of AI in Innovation and Productivity

The integration of AI into business processes can significantly boost innovation and productivity. Companies that use AI for data analysis can quickly identify trends and adapt their product development strategies accordingly. AI can also help businesses to customize products for different market segments, increasing their appeal and market share.

On the productivity front, AI-driven tools can manage and analyze large datasets more efficiently than humans, leading to faster decision-making and reduced downtime. AI can also predict equipment failures before they occur, minimizing maintenance times and improving overall operational efficiency.

Case Studies of AI in Innovation and Productivity

A tech company used AI to revolutionize its product design process. By employing generative design algorithms, the company was able to explore thousands of potential designs quickly, resulting in a groundbreaking new product that outperformed competitors.

Another case study involves a logistics company that implemented AI to optimize its delivery routes. The AI system analyzed traffic patterns, weather conditions, and delivery windows to suggest the most efficient routes, significantly reducing delivery times and fuel consumption.

AI in Customer Experience

Understanding AI in Customer Experience

AI has the potential to transform customer experience by providing personalized and seamless interactions. Through the use of chatbots, recommendation systems, and personalized marketing, AI can engage customers in a more meaningful way. AI systems can analyze customer data, including past purchases and browsing history, to predict future needs and preferences.

This level of personalization can lead to a more satisfying customer journey, as businesses can anticipate needs and resolve issues before they become problems. AI also enables omnichannel support, ensuring that customers receive consistent service across various platforms.

Benefits of AI in Customer Experience

By leveraging AI, businesses can achieve a higher level of customer satisfaction, leading to increased loyalty and retention. AI-driven insights can help companies to tailor their communications and offers, making customers feel understood and valued. Additionally, AI can reduce response times and improve the accuracy of customer service interactions.

AI also allows for the collection and analysis of customer feedback on a large scale, enabling businesses to quickly adapt and improve their products and services. This proactive approach to customer experience can significantly enhance a company's reputation and competitive position.

Case Studies of AI in Customer Experience

A leading e-commerce platform used AI to enhance its recommendation engine, resulting in a significant increase in sales. By analyzing customer data, the AI system was able to suggest products that customers were more likely to purchase, improving the shopping experience and increasing revenue.

In the hospitality industry, a hotel chain implemented AI to personalize guest experiences. The AI system used guest preferences and behavior to offer customized room settings, dining options, and activities, leading to higher guest satisfaction and repeat visits.

Famous Quotes

"The business plans of the next 10,000 startups are easy to forecast: Take X and add AI." - Kevin Kelly, Co-Founder of Wired Magazine

"Artificial Intelligence, deep learning, machine learning —

whatever you're doing if you don't understand it — learn it. Because otherwise you're going to be a dinosaur within 3 years."
- Mark Cuban, Entrepreneur and Investor

AI in Market Differentiation

Understanding AI in Market Differentiation

Market differentiation is crucial for businesses to stand out in a crowded marketplace. AI can be a key differentiator by enabling companies to offer unique products, services, and customer experiences. By harnessing the power of AI, businesses can identify niche markets, tailor their offerings, and deliver superior value to customers.

AI can also help companies to innovate at a faster pace, staying ahead of competitors. Through predictive analytics, businesses can anticipate market shifts and adapt their strategies accordingly, ensuring they remain relevant and competitive.

Benefits of AI in Market Differentiation

AI-driven market differentiation can lead to a stronger brand identity and a more loyal customer base. By offering personalized experiences and innovative products, companies can create a unique value proposition that is difficult for competitors to replicate. AI also enables businesses to respond quickly to changing consumer demands, maintaining their market position.

Furthermore, AI can enhance a company's reputation as a leader in technology and innovation, attracting customers who value cutting-edge solutions. This can open up new revenue streams and expand market reach.

Case Studies of AI in Market Differentiation

A fashion retailer used AI to offer a virtual fitting room experience online, allowing customers to see how clothes would look on their avatars. This innovative use of AI set the retailer apart from competitors and resulted in a significant increase in online sales.

An automotive company integrated AI into its vehicles to provide advanced driver-assistance systems. This not only improved safety features but also positioned the company as a pioneer in AI-enhanced driving, differentiating it from other car manufacturers.

AI in Cost Efficiency

Understanding AI in Cost Efficiency

Cost efficiency is a critical factor in maintaining a competitive advantage. AI can contribute to cost savings by optimizing business processes, reducing waste, and improving resource management. AI algorithms can analyze operational data to identify inefficiencies and suggest improvements.

AI can also automate routine tasks, such as data entry and analysis, which reduces labor costs and minimizes human error. In manufacturing, AI can optimize production schedules and maintenance routines, ensuring that equipment runs at peak efficiency and reducing downtime.

Benefits of AI in Cost Efficiency

The adoption of AI can lead to significant cost reductions across various business functions. By automating processes, companies can scale their operations without a proportional increase in costs. AI can also help businesses make better use of their resources, such as raw materials and energy, leading to further savings.

Additionally, AI can improve the accuracy of forecasting,

allowing businesses to better manage inventory and reduce holding costs. This level of precision in resource allocation can be a game-changer for companies looking to improve their bottom line.

Case Studies of AI in Cost Efficiency

A multinational corporation implemented AI in its procurement process, which helped it to negotiate better terms with suppliers and reduce procurement costs by a significant margin. The AI system analyzed historical data and market conditions to suggest the optimal timing and quantity for purchases.

In the energy sector, a utility company used AI to predict demand patterns and optimize the distribution of electricity. This resulted in reduced energy waste, lower operational costs, and a smaller carbon footprint.

Future of AI in Competitive Advantage

Emerging AI Technologies in Competitive Advantage

The future of AI in competitive advantage lies in the continuous development of new technologies and applications. Quantum computing, for example, has the potential to process data at unprecedented speeds, opening up new possibilities for AI algorithms. Edge computing is another area that can enhance AI by processing data closer to the source, reducing latency and improving real-time decision-making.

Augmented reality (AR) and virtual reality (VR) combined with AI can create immersive experiences for customers, revolutionizing industries such as retail, real estate, and education. The integration of AI with the Internet of Things (IoT) can lead to smarter, more connected products and services, further differentiating companies in the market.

Ethical Considerations in AI Competitive Advantage

As AI technologies advance, ethical considerations become increasingly important. Companies must ensure that their use of AI aligns with ethical standards and societal values. This includes addressing issues such as data privacy, bias in AI algorithms, and the impact of automation on employment.

Businesses must be transparent about their use of AI and work to build trust with consumers and stakeholders. They should also engage in responsible AI practices, such as implementing fairness checks and ensuring that AI systems are explainable and accountable.

AI in Competitive Advantage: Opportunities and Challenges

The opportunities presented by AI in competitive advantage are vast, but they also come with challenges. Companies must navigate the complexities of integrating AI into their operations, including the need for skilled personnel, data management, and the potential for disruption to existing business models.

To capitalize on the opportunities, businesses must stay abreast of technological developments and be willing to invest in AI research and development. They must also be agile, adapting their strategies as AI technologies evolve. By overcoming these challenges, companies can harness the power of AI to gain a significant competitive edge in the marketplace.

Review Questions

1. How can AI contribute to business strategy?
2. What is a key benefit of AI in innovation and productivity?
3. How can AI enhance customer experience?
4. What role can AI play in market differentiation?
5. How can AI contribute to cost efficiency in a business?
6. What are some benefits of incorporating AI in business strategy?
7. How can AI contribute to innovation and productivity in a business?
8. What are some ethical considerations when using AI for competitive advantage?

CHAPTER 14

AI and Entrepreneurship

The advent of artificial intelligence (AI) has revolutionized the way startups are created and developed. AI in startup creation involves leveraging machine learning algorithms, natural language processing, and other AI technologies to streamline the process of launching a new business. From market research and business planning to product development and customer acquisition, AI tools can assist entrepreneurs in making data-driven decisions and automating repetitive tasks.

For instance, AI can analyze vast amounts of market data to identify trends and opportunities that might be missed by human analysis. Additionally, AI-powered virtual assistants can help manage schedules, set reminders, and even draft emails, allowing founders to focus on strategic tasks. The use of AI in startup creation not only enhances efficiency but also provides a competitive edge in a fast-paced entrepreneurial environment.

Benefits of AI in Startup Creation

The benefits of AI in startup creation are multifaceted. AI can significantly reduce the time and resources required to perform market analysis, enabling startups to quickly pivot and adapt to changing market conditions. Moreover, AI-driven analytics can provide insights into customer behavior, helping startups tailor their products and services to meet specific needs. By automating routine tasks, AI allows entrepreneurs to concentrate on core business activities, such as strategy and innovation.

Another key benefit is the personalization capabilities that AI offers. Startups can use AI to deliver personalized experiences to their customers, which can lead to increased customer satisfaction and loyalty. Additionally, AI can help startups manage risks by predicting potential challenges and suggesting mitigation strategies. Overall, AI empowers startups to operate more effectively and scale their businesses with greater precision.

Case Studies of AI in Startup Creation

One notable case study involves a fintech startup that used AI to disrupt the traditional banking industry. By implementing AI algorithms, the startup was able to offer personalized financial advice to users, automate investment portfolio management, and provide real-time fraud detection. This not only streamlined the user experience but also allowed the startup to operate with a leaner team and lower overhead costs.

Another example is a healthcare startup that developed an AI-powered diagnostic tool. The tool uses machine learning to analyze medical images and assist doctors in identifying diseases at an early stage. This startup was able to enter the market rapidly by leveraging AI to enhance the accuracy and speed of diagnosis, thereby gaining a competitive advantage in the healthcare sector.

AI in Business Model Innovation

Understanding AI in Business

Model Innovation

Business model innovation is about rethinking the fundamental approach to creating, delivering, and capturing value. AI plays a crucial role in this process by enabling startups to explore new ways of serving customers and operating their businesses. AI technologies can uncover hidden patterns in data, predict customer preferences, and optimize operations, leading to innovative business models that were previously inconceivable.

For example, AI can facilitate the creation of subscription-based models by predicting which customers are likely to subscribe and what pricing strategies will be most effective. It can also enable the sharing economy by optimizing the allocation of resources and matching supply with demand in real-time. By integrating AI into their business models, startups can achieve higher levels of customization and efficiency.

Benefits of AI in Business Model Innovation

The integration of AI into business models can lead to significant cost savings, as it allows for the automation of various processes that would otherwise require manual labor. Additionally, AI can drive revenue growth by enabling more targeted marketing and sales strategies. It can also create new revenue streams by identifying untapped market segments or by enhancing existing products and services with AI features.

Furthermore, AI can contribute to sustainability by optimizing resource usage and reducing waste. For instance, AI can improve energy efficiency in manufacturing or help design circular economy business models where products are designed for reuse and recycling. The adaptability and scalability of AI-driven business models provide startups with the agility needed to thrive in dynamic markets.

Case Studies of AI in Business Model Innovation

A prominent case study is an e-commerce startup that used AI to personalize the shopping experience. By analyzing customer data, the startup was able to offer personalized product recommendations, optimize inventory management, and streamline logistics. This AI-driven approach resulted in increased customer engagement and a significant boost in sales.

Another case involves a startup in the energy sector that developed an AI-based platform for monitoring and managing energy consumption. The platform allows businesses and consumers to track their energy usage in real-time and receive suggestions for reducing costs and carbon footprint. This innovative business model has not only attracted environmentally conscious customers but also paved the way for new partnerships and growth opportunities.

Quick Facts & Statistics

AI in Business: By the Numbers

AI and Customer Engagement

AI and the Environment

AI in Funding and Investment

Understanding AI in Funding and Investment

Securing funding and managing investments are critical aspects of entrepreneurship. AI is transforming these areas by providing tools for better decision-making and risk assessment. Startups can use AI to analyze investment opportunities, predict market trends, and attract potential investors by showcasing data-driven business plans and projections.

AI can also assist investors in identifying promising startups by evaluating their potential for success based on various metrics, such as market size, team experience, and technological innovation. By leveraging AI, both startups and investors can make more informed choices, leading to more successful funding rounds and investment outcomes.

Benefits of AI in Funding and Investment

For startups, AI can streamline the fundraising process by identifying the most suitable investors and tailoring pitches to their specific interests. AI-driven analysis can also help startups understand the valuation of their company and negotiate better terms. For investors, AI provides a comprehensive analysis of market conditions and startup performance, reducing the time and effort required to evaluate investment opportunities.

Additionally, AI can monitor the financial health of a startup in real-time, providing early warning signs of potential issues that could affect investment returns. This proactive approach to investment management can lead to more stable and profitable portfolios.

Case Studies of AI in Funding and Investment

A case study worth mentioning is a startup that developed an AI-powered platform for connecting entrepreneurs with investors. The platform uses machine learning algorithms to match startups with investors based on compatibility in investment thesis, industry focus, and funding stage. This has resulted in more efficient and successful funding rounds for participating startups.

Another example is a venture capital firm that utilizes AI to screen and evaluate potential investments. The firm's AI system analyzes thousands of data points, including market trends, financial performance, and team expertise, to predict the likelihood of a startup's success. This data-driven approach has enabled the firm to make quicker and more accurate investment decisions.

Think & Reflect

Consider the Power of AI: The examples provided illustrate how AI can streamline processes and improve decision-making in the investment sector. Reflect on how these AI applications could be applied to other areas of business. How might AI transform your industry?

AI and Decision-Making: The venture capital firm uses AI to analyze data and predict a startup's likelihood of success. How do you think this compares to traditional methods of decision-making? What are the potential benefits and drawbacks of relying on AI for such decisions?

AI and Efficiency: The AI-powered platform for connecting entrepreneurs with investors has made funding rounds more efficient. Can you think of other business processes that could be made more efficient with AI? What might be the potential challenges in implementing such solutions?

Future of AI: AI is already making a significant impact in the business world. What do you think the future holds for AI in business? How might businesses need to adapt to stay competitive in an increasingly AI-driven world?

AI in Market Entry

Understanding AI in Market Entry

Market entry is a critical phase for any startup, and AI can significantly enhance the process. AI tools can help startups identify the most promising markets, understand local consumer behavior, and develop entry strategies that are tailored to specific market conditions. AI can also simulate different market scenarios, allowing startups to test their strategies before actual deployment.

By analyzing social media, online forums, and customer reviews, AI can provide insights into consumer sentiment and preferences, which can inform product development and marketing campaigns. Additionally, AI can optimize pricing strategies by taking into account factors such as competition, demand elasticity, and consumer purchasing power.

Benefits of AI in Market Entry

AI enables startups to enter new markets with a data-driven approach, reducing the risks associated with market entry. It allows for more accurate targeting of customer segments and more effective allocation of marketing resources. AI can also help startups quickly adapt to changing market dynamics, ensuring that their entry strategies remain relevant and effective.

Moreover, AI can automate language translation and cultural adaptation of marketing materials, making it easier for startups to communicate with customers in different regions. This level of customization and responsiveness can lead to higher customer acquisition rates and faster market penetration.

Case Studies of AI in Market Entry

A notable case study involves a retail startup that used AI to analyze consumer behavior patterns across different regions. By understanding local preferences, the startup was able to tailor its product offerings and marketing messages, resulting in a successful market entry and rapid establishment of a loyal customer base.

Another case study features a tech startup that leveraged AI to optimize its app localization process. The AI system analyzed user feedback from different countries to prioritize features and interface adjustments. This approach allowed the startup to effectively cater to local tastes and preferences, driving user adoption and engagement in each new market.

AI in Growth and Scaling

Understanding AI in Growth and Scaling

Growth and scaling are pivotal stages in a startup's lifecycle, and AI can play a significant role in ensuring successful expansion. AI can help startups identify growth opportunities, optimize operations for scale, and maintain customer satisfaction as the business grows. By analyzing internal and external data, AI can forecast demand, optimize resource allocation, and streamline supply chain processes.

AI can also assist in scaling customer service operations by deploying chatbots and automated support systems that can handle a large volume of inquiries without compromising quality. Furthermore, AI-driven personalization can help startups maintain a high level of customer engagement even as their customer base expands.

Benefits of AI in Growth and Scaling

The use of AI in growth and scaling enables startups to maintain operational efficiency and high service levels despite increasing complexity. AI can automate repetitive tasks, allowing human employees to focus on strategic initiatives and creative problem-solving. This not only improves productivity but also supports a positive work culture during periods of rapid change.

Additionally, AI can help startups manage the financial aspects of scaling by providing insights into cash flow, expenses, and revenue projections. This financial clarity is essential for making informed decisions about investments, hiring, and expansion plans. AI's ability to adapt to new data and learn from outcomes ensures that startups remain agile and responsive as they grow.

Case Studies of AI in Growth and Scaling

A case study that illustrates the impact of AI on scaling involves an e-commerce startup that implemented AI-driven demand forecasting and inventory management. This allowed the startup to optimize stock levels, reduce waste, and improve delivery times, which was crucial for customer satisfaction and retention during a period of rapid growth.

Another example is a software-as-a-service (SaaS) startup that used AI to enhance its customer success platform. The AI system provided personalized recommendations to users based on their usage patterns, leading to increased engagement and a higher lifetime value per customer. This scalable, AI-powered approach supported the startup's growth trajectory and helped it establish a strong market presence.

Future of AI in Entrepreneurship

Emerging AI Technologies in

Entrepreneurship

The future of AI in entrepreneurship is marked by continuous innovation and the emergence of new technologies. Advancements in AI such as generative adversarial networks (GANs), reinforcement learning, and quantum computing are set to open up new possibilities for startups. These technologies can lead to the creation of more sophisticated products and services, as well as the discovery of novel business models.

For example, GANs can be used to generate realistic images and videos, which can be leveraged for marketing purposes or to create virtual prototypes of products. Reinforcement learning can optimize business processes by continuously learning from interactions with the environment. Quantum computing, although still in its infancy, has the potential to solve complex problems at unprecedented speeds, which could revolutionize data analysis and decision-making in startups.

Ethical Considerations in AI Entrepreneurship

As AI technologies become more integrated into entrepreneurship, ethical considerations must be addressed. Issues such as data privacy, algorithmic bias, and transparency are of paramount importance. Startups must ensure that their AI systems are designed and implemented in a way that respects user privacy and prevents discrimination. Transparency in AI decision-making processes is also crucial for building trust with customers and stakeholders.

Entrepreneurs have a responsibility to consider the societal impact of their AI applications and to engage in ethical practices. This includes being transparent about data usage, ensuring fairness in AI outcomes, and being accountable for the consequences of AI-driven decisions. By prioritizing ethics, startups can contribute to the development of AI in a manner that is beneficial and sustainable for society.

AI in Entrepreneurship: Opportunities and Challenges

The opportunities presented by AI in entrepreneurship are vast. AI can enable startups to operate with greater efficiency, innovate at a faster pace, and provide exceptional value to customers. However, challenges such as ensuring data quality, managing AI integration, and addressing ethical concerns must be overcome. Startups must also navigate the competitive landscape, as AI levels the playing field and allows new entrants to challenge established players.

To capitalize on the opportunities and address the challenges, startups need to invest in AI talent, foster a culture of continuous learning, and stay abreast of technological advancements. Collaboration with other startups, academic institutions, and industry experts can also provide valuable insights and resources. As the AI landscape evolves, entrepreneurs who are adaptable, innovative, and ethical will be well-positioned to succeed.

Review Questions

1. What is one of the benefits of AI in startup creation?
2. How can AI contribute to business model innovation?
3. What role can AI play in funding and investment for startups?
4. How can AI assist in market entry for startups?
5. What is one of the future considerations for AI in entrepreneurship?
6. What are some benefits of incorporating AI in startup creation?
7. How can AI contribute to business model innovation?
8. What are some potential challenges and ethical considerations when incorporating AI in entrepreneurship?

CHAPTER 15

AI and Business Ethics

Data privacy is a critical concern in the age of artificial intelligence (AI). AI systems often require vast amounts of data to learn and make decisions. This data can include personal information that, if mishandled, could lead to privacy breaches. Understanding AI's impact on data privacy involves recognizing how AI collects, processes, and stores personal data, as well as the potential for AI to enhance or compromise data protection measures.

AI technologies can be used to protect data privacy through encryption, anomaly detection, and automated compliance with data protection regulations. However, they can also pose risks when algorithms process sensitive information without proper safeguards, leading to unintended exposure of personal data.

Benefits and Risks of AI in Data Privacy

Benefits: AI can significantly enhance data privacy by automating the detection of security breaches and providing more robust encryption methods. AI-driven systems can analyze large datasets to identify and rectify vulnerabilities, potentially preventing data leaks before they occur. Additionally, AI can help organizations comply with data protection regulations by automatically classifying and handling personal data according to legal requirements.

Risks: On the flip side, AI systems themselves can become targets for cyber-attacks, leading to massive data breaches. If an AI system is compromised, the scale of data exposure can be extensive. Moreover, AI algorithms may inadvertently reveal personal information through data inference, where sensitive details are deduced from seemingly innocuous data.

Case Studies of AI and Data Privacy

One notable case study involves a healthcare organization that used AI to predict patient health outcomes. While the AI system improved care, it also raised concerns about patient data privacy, as it required access to detailed medical records. The organization implemented strict access controls and data anonymization techniques to protect patient privacy while still benefiting from AI insights.

Another case study focuses on a retail company that used AI for personalized marketing. The AI analyzed customer behavior to tailor promotions, but it inadvertently exposed shopping habits that customers considered private. The company had to revise its data handling practices and provide clearer consent mechanisms to address privacy concerns.

Quick Facts & Statistics

AI in Healthcare:

AI in Retail:

AI and Data Privacy:

AI and Bias

Understanding AI and Bias

Bias in AI refers to systematic errors in data processing that lead to unfair outcomes, such as favoring one group over another. AI systems learn from data, and if that data contains biases, the AI's decisions will reflect those biases. Understanding AI and bias involves examining the sources of bias, which can stem from skewed datasets, prejudiced human input, or flawed algorithm design.

It is essential to identify and mitigate bias in AI to ensure fair and ethical decision-making. This can involve diversifying training datasets, developing algorithms that detect and correct for bias, and continuously monitoring AI systems for biased behavior.

Benefits and Risks of AI in Bias

Benefits: When properly managed, AI can help reduce human biases by providing objective, data-driven decisions. AI can also be used to identify and mitigate existing biases within large datasets, promoting fairer outcomes across various applications, from hiring practices to loan approvals.

Risks: However, AI can also perpetuate and amplify biases if not carefully designed and monitored. Biased AI systems can lead to discriminatory practices, such as racial profiling or gender discrimination, which can have severe legal and social repercussions for businesses.

Case Studies of AI and Bias

A significant case study involves an AI recruiting tool that was found to be biased against female applicants. The tool learned from historical hiring data that favored men, leading to a gender-biased selection process. The company had to halt the tool's use and implement measures to ensure future AI systems would not replicate such biases.

Another case study is a credit scoring AI system that unfairly disadvantaged minority groups. The algorithm used zip codes as a factor, which correlated with racial demographics, leading to lower credit scores for individuals from certain areas. The financial institution responsible for the AI system faced legal challenges and had to redesign the algorithm to prevent such bias.

AI and Transparency

Understanding AI and Transparency

Transparency in AI involves the ability to understand and trace how AI systems make decisions. It is crucial for ensuring accountability and trust in AI technologies. Transparent AI systems allow users to comprehend the rationale behind decisions, which is particularly important in sectors where those decisions have significant consequences, such as healthcare, finance, and law enforcement.

Achieving transparency can be challenging, especially with complex models like deep neural networks, which are often considered "black boxes" due to their inscrutable decision-making processes. Efforts to increase AI transparency include developing explainable AI (XAI) models and providing clear documentation of AI systems' inner workings.

Benefits and Risks of AI in Transparency

Benefits: Transparent AI systems foster trust and facilitate user acceptance. They also enable regulatory compliance, as businesses can demonstrate how their AI systems align with legal and ethical standards. Furthermore, transparency allows for the identification and correction of errors or biases within AI systems.

Risks: Lack of transparency can lead to mistrust and resistance to AI adoption. It can also pose risks to individuals affected by AI decisions, as they may not have recourse to challenge or understand those decisions. Additionally, opaque AI systems can make it difficult to diagnose and fix issues, potentially leading to persistent errors and biases.

Case Studies of AI and Transparency

A case study in the financial sector highlights a bank that implemented an AI system for loan approvals. The bank faced criticism when customers complained about unexplained loan rejections. In response, the bank adopted an XAI approach, providing customers with clear explanations for the AI's decisions, which improved customer satisfaction and trust.

Another case study involves a law enforcement agency that used AI for predictive policing. The lack of transparency around how the AI identified high-risk areas led to public concern over potential bias and privacy violations. The agency had to work on making the AI's decision-making process more transparent to the public to maintain its legitimacy and community trust.

AI and Accountability

Understanding AI and Accountability

Accountability in AI refers to the assignment of responsibility for the outcomes of AI systems. As AI becomes more autonomous, determining who is accountable for its actions—whether it be the developers, users, or the AI itself—becomes increasingly complex. Understanding AI and accountability involves establishing clear guidelines and frameworks that outline who is responsible for the AI's decisions and the consequences of those decisions.

Ensuring accountability is essential for maintaining public trust and for legal compliance. It requires mechanisms for tracking decision-making processes, auditing AI systems, and providing remedies when AI causes harm or operates outside of acceptable parameters.

Benefits and Risks of AI in Accountability

Benefits: Clear accountability structures for AI can lead to more responsible development and use of AI technologies. They ensure that AI systems are used ethically and that there are consequences for misuse or harmful outcomes. This can prevent harm and promote trust in AI applications.

Risks: Without clear accountability, it can be challenging to address the negative impacts of AI, such as privacy breaches or discriminatory decisions. This can result in legal and reputational damage for businesses and harm to individuals affected by the AI's actions.

Case Studies of AI and Accountability

In one case study, an autonomous vehicle was involved in a collision, raising questions about liability. The investigation focused on whether the fault lay with the vehicle's AI system, the vehicle's manufacturer, or the human operator. The case highlighted the need for clear accountability guidelines in the age of autonomous machines.

Another case study examines a social media platform that used AI to moderate content. When the AI erroneously flagged and removed legitimate content, the platform had to address who was accountable for the mistake—the AI developers, the platform, or the AI itself. The platform implemented a review process to handle such errors and clarify accountability.

AI and Employee Rights

Understanding AI and Employee Rights

AI's impact on employee rights encompasses issues such as workplace surveillance, job displacement due to automation, and AI in decision-making processes that affect employees, like promotions or terminations. Understanding AI and employee rights involves examining how AI technologies can be used in ways that respect and protect the rights of workers.

Employers must balance the benefits of AI, such as increased productivity and efficiency, with the ethical considerations of how AI applications affect their workforce. This includes ensuring transparency, fairness, and privacy in AI-driven workplace practices.

Benefits and Risks of AI in Employee Rights

Benefits: AI can improve working conditions by automating mundane tasks, thus freeing employees to focus on more meaningful work. AI can also support fairer decision-making by providing objective data analysis, potentially reducing human biases in evaluations and promotions.

Risks: However, AI can also pose risks to employee rights, such as invasive monitoring that infringes on privacy or algorithmic management that leads to unfair treatment. Additionally, AI-driven automation can result in job displacement if not managed with a focus on retraining and reskilling employees.

Case Studies of AI and Employee Rights

A case study in the retail industry illustrates a company that implemented AI for scheduling shifts. While the AI optimized staffing levels, it also led to unpredictable schedules for employees, affecting their work-life balance. The company had to revise its AI system to consider employee preferences and rights.

Another case study involves a manufacturing firm that used AI for performance monitoring. The AI collected data on employee movements and productivity, but workers raised concerns about privacy and the pressure of constant surveillance. The firm had to develop a policy that balanced productivity monitoring with respect for employee privacy.

Test Your Knowledge

Let's see how well you understood the concepts in this section. Try to answer the following questions:

1. What was the primary issue with the AI system used for scheduling shifts in the retail industry case study?
2. How did the company in the retail industry case study

address the problem with their AI system?

3. In the manufacturing firm case study, what concerns did the employees raise about the AI system used for performance monitoring?

Remember: AI can be a powerful tool for businesses, but it's crucial to balance efficiency and productivity with respect for employee rights and privacy.

Future of AI in Business Ethics

Emerging AI Technologies and Business Ethics

As AI technologies continue to evolve, they bring new ethical considerations for businesses. Emerging technologies like affective computing, which enables AI to interpret human emotions, and advanced predictive analytics, which can forecast individual behavior, raise questions about consent, autonomy, and the manipulation of behavior.

Businesses must stay informed about these emerging technologies and proactively address the ethical implications they bring. This includes engaging with stakeholders, including ethicists and the public, to ensure that AI development aligns with societal values and ethical norms.

Ethical Considerations in AI Business Ethics

Ethical considerations in AI business ethics revolve around principles such as beneficence, non-maleficence, autonomy, justice, and explicability. Businesses must consider the potential impacts of AI on stakeholders and work to prevent harm, ensure fairness, and maintain transparency in their AI applications.

This involves implementing ethical guidelines for AI use, conducting impact assessments, and establishing governance structures to oversee AI ethics within the organization.

AI in Business Ethics: Opportunities and Challenges

The integration of AI into business practices offers opportunities to enhance ethical decision-making, improve stakeholder engagement, and foster trust. AI can help businesses identify and address ethical issues more effectively, leading to better outcomes for both the company and society.

However, challenges remain, including keeping pace with the rapid development of AI technologies, ensuring diverse and inclusive perspectives in AI design, and maintaining an ongoing dialogue about the ethical use of AI. Businesses must be willing to invest in ethical AI practices and be prepared to adapt as new ethical challenges arise.

The ethical landscape of AI in business is complex and ever-changing. As AI becomes more ingrained in business operations, the need for ethical vigilance grows. Companies that prioritize ethical considerations in their AI strategies will be better positioned to navigate this landscape and harness the full potential of AI in a responsible and beneficial manner.

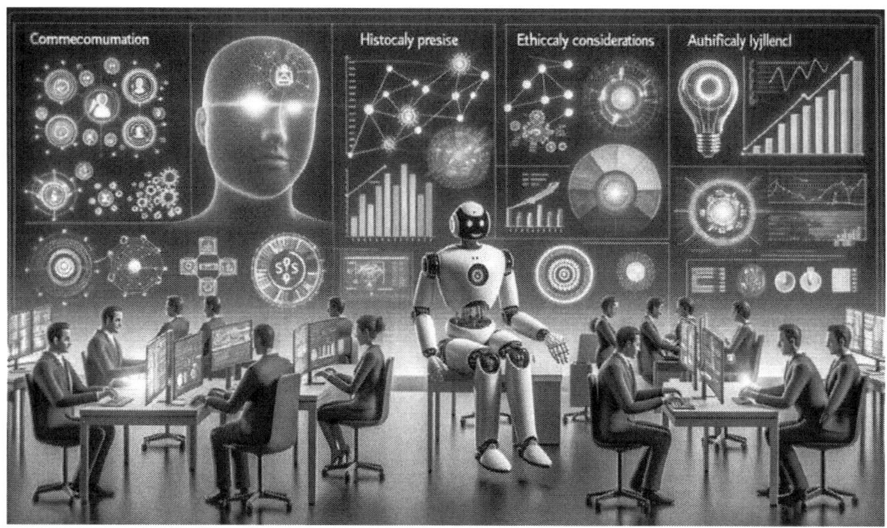

Review Questions

1. What is a potential risk of AI in data privacy?
2. What is a significant concern regarding AI and bias?
3. Why is transparency important in AI?
4. What does accountability in AI refer to?
5. How can AI potentially impact employee rights?

CHAPTER 16

AI and Legal Implications

Intellectual property (IP) rights are legal protections granted to creators for their inventions and artistic works. In the context of artificial intelligence (AI), IP rights become complex due to the autonomous nature of AI systems. AI can create new works or inventions that challenge traditional notions of authorship and ownership. The question arises: who owns the IP of a work created by AI? Is it the developer, the user, the owner of the AI system, or the AI itself? These questions are at the forefront of legal discussions as AI technology continues to advance.

There are several types of IP rights that can be associated with AI, including patents, copyrights, trademarks, and trade secrets. Patents protect inventions, which may include AI algorithms or systems. Copyrights protect original works of authorship, such as literature, music, and software code. Trademarks protect brand identities, including logos and slogans. Trade secrets protect confidential business information that provides a competitive edge.

Legal Issues in AI and Intellectual Property Rights

The legal issues surrounding AI and IP rights are multifaceted. One major issue is the patentability of AI-generated inventions. Traditionally, patents are granted to human inventors, but as AI systems become more capable of inventing, the definition of an "inventor" is being questioned. Copyright law also faces challenges, as it is unclear whether AI-generated content can be copyrighted and, if so, who the copyright holder would be. Trademarks and trade secrets involving AI also raise questions about ownership and infringement in scenarios where AI autonomously creates or uses such protected materials.

Another significant issue is the liability for infringement of IP rights by AI. If an AI system infringes on existing IP rights, determining who is responsible—the developer, the user, or the owner—becomes a legal challenge. Additionally, the cross-border nature of AI technology complicates the enforcement of IP rights, as different countries have varying laws and regulations.

Case Studies of AI and Intellectual Property Rights

One notable case study involves an AI system named "DABUS" that created two inventions. The AI's creator, Dr. Stephen Thaler, filed for patents listing DABUS as the inventor. The patent offices in the UK, EU, and US initially rejected the applications, stating that an inventor must be a natural person. However, this case has sparked a global debate on the need to adapt IP laws to accommodate AI-generated inventions.

Another case study is the use of AI in creating artworks. An AI-generated artwork was sold at auction for a substantial sum, raising questions about copyright ownership. The developers of the AI claimed ownership, but this has been debated by legal experts who argue that the AI should be considered the author.

AI and Data Protection Laws

Understanding AI and Data Protection Laws

Data protection laws are designed to safeguard individuals' personal data and ensure that organizations that collect, process, and store such data do so responsibly and transparently. AI systems often rely on vast amounts of data, including personal data, to learn and make decisions. This reliance places AI at the center of data protection concerns. Compliance with data protection laws, such as the General Data Protection Regulation (GDPR) in the European Union, is crucial for businesses utilizing AI.

Key principles of data protection laws that impact AI include data minimization, purpose limitation, data accuracy, and individuals' rights to access, rectify, and erase their data. AI systems must be designed and operated in a way that respects these principles and the privacy of individuals.

Legal Issues in AI and Data Protection Laws

AI poses several legal issues in relation to data protection laws. One of the most significant is the challenge of ensuring transparency and explainability in AI decision-making processes. Data subjects have the right to understand how their data is being used and how decisions that affect them are made. However, the complexity of AI algorithms can make it difficult to provide clear explanations, potentially violating data protection laws.

Another issue is the potential for AI to process personal data beyond the scope for which consent was given, infringing on the principle of purpose limitation. Additionally, AI's predictive capabilities may lead to decisions based on inaccurate or biased data, resulting in harm to individuals and non-compliance with data accuracy requirements.

Case Studies of AI and Data Protection Laws

A case study highlighting the intersection of AI and data protection is the use of facial recognition technology. Several cities and organizations have faced legal challenges for using AI-powered facial recognition without adequate consent or transparency, leading to privacy violations under data protection laws.

Another case involves a company that used AI for hiring purposes. The AI system screened applicants' social media profiles, potentially processing personal data beyond what was necessary for the hiring process. This raised concerns under data protection laws, leading to legal scrutiny and the need for the company to revise its AI practices.

Did You Know?

AI and Privacy

Artificial Intelligence (AI) has the potential to significantly impact privacy. AI systems can process vast amounts of data, including personal data, which can lead to privacy concerns. For example, AI-powered facial recognition technology can identify individuals in public spaces, potentially without their consent.

AI and Legal Implications

As AI continues to evolve, so does the legal landscape. Laws are being developed and updated to address the unique challenges posed by AI, particularly in the areas of data protection and privacy. For example, the European Union's General Data Protection Regulation (GDPR) includes provisions specifically addressing AI and data protection.

AI and Employment Laws

Understanding AI and Employment Laws

Employment laws govern the relationship between employers and employees, including hiring practices, workplace discrimination, and termination. AI is increasingly used in various aspects of employment, from recruitment to performance evaluations. While AI can streamline HR processes, it also raises legal concerns regarding compliance with employment laws.

For instance, AI tools used in recruitment must not discriminate against candidates based on protected characteristics such as race, gender, or age. Similarly, AI-driven performance management systems must be fair and unbiased to comply with employment laws.

Legal Issues in AI and Employment Laws

One of the primary legal issues with AI in employment is the potential for algorithmic bias, which can lead to discriminatory hiring or evaluation practices. Even if unintentional, such bias can result in violations of anti-discrimination laws. Employers must ensure that AI tools are designed and implemented in a way that prevents discrimination and promotes fairness.

Another issue is the use of AI in monitoring employee productivity and behavior. While employers have a legitimate interest in monitoring work performance, excessive surveillance through AI may infringe on employees' privacy rights and lead to legal challenges.

Case Studies of AI and Employment Laws

A notable case study involves an AI recruitment tool that was found to be biased against female candidates. The company using the tool faced legal action for gender discrimination and had to overhaul its recruitment process to ensure compliance with employment laws.

Another case study is the use of AI for employee monitoring. A lawsuit was filed against an employer for using AI to track employees' keystrokes and screen time without proper disclosure, violating privacy regulations and employment laws.

AI and Consumer Protection Laws

Understanding AI and Consumer Protection Laws

Consumer protection laws are designed to protect consumers from unfair, deceptive, or fraudulent business practices. AI technologies that interact with consumers, such as recommendation systems or personalized advertising, must adhere to these laws. The use of AI must not mislead consumers or result in unfair treatment.

Transparency is a key aspect of consumer protection laws, and businesses must clearly disclose how AI is used in their products or services. Consumers should be informed about the data being collected and the logic behind AI-driven recommendations or decisions that affect them.

Legal Issues in AI and Consumer Protection Laws

AI raises several legal issues under consumer protection laws. One issue is the potential for AI to engage in price discrimination, offering different prices to consumers based on their behavior or demographics. This practice may be considered unfair and violate consumer protection laws.

Another issue is the accuracy of AI-generated claims or descriptions of products and services. If AI provides inaccurate or misleading information, it could lead to consumer deception and legal repercussions for the business.

Case Studies of AI and Consumer Protection Laws

A case study involving AI and consumer protection is a travel booking website that used AI to personalize prices. The website faced legal scrutiny for potentially discriminating against consumers based on their browsing history and purchasing power.

Another case involves an AI-powered health app that claimed to diagnose medical conditions. The app provided incorrect diagnoses, leading to a lawsuit for misleading consumers and violating consumer protection laws.

Biographical Snapshot

Dr. Latanya Sweeney

Dr. Latanya Sweeney is a renowned computer scientist, professor, and researcher in the field of data privacy. She is known for her groundbreaking work on the implications of AI and consumer protection laws.

Education and Career

Contributions to AI and Consumer Protection

Dr. Sweeney's research has significantly influenced the understanding of how AI can impact consumer protection. Her work has led to the development of new standards and regulations to ensure that AI technologies are used ethically and responsibly.

AI and Competition Laws

Understanding AI and Competition Laws

Competition laws, also known as antitrust laws, are designed to prevent anti-competitive practices and promote fair competition in the marketplace. AI can impact competition in various ways, such as through algorithmic pricing, market manipulation, or collusion between AI systems. Businesses using AI must ensure that their practices do not violate competition laws.

AI can also contribute to market concentration if a few companies control the AI technology and data, potentially leading to monopolistic practices. Regulators are increasingly focused on how AI affects competition and are exploring ways to adapt antitrust laws to the digital age.

Legal Issues in AI and Competition Laws

One of the legal issues with AI in the context of competition laws is the potential for algorithmic collusion. AI systems may independently learn to set prices at a non-competitive level, which could be seen as a form of tacit collusion. This raises questions about how to apply traditional antitrust concepts to AI behavior.

Another issue is the use of AI to engage in predatory pricing or exclusionary practices, which could harm competition and consumer choice. Regulators are examining how to address these challenges and ensure that AI is used in a way that supports healthy competition.

Case Studies of AI and Competition Laws

A case study in this area involves online retailers using AI for dynamic pricing. Some of these retailers were investigated for using AI to monitor competitors' prices and automatically adjust their own prices, potentially leading to anti-competitive behavior.

Another case study is the acquisition of AI startups by large tech companies. These acquisitions have come under scrutiny from competition authorities, concerned about the consolidation of AI technology and data, which could stifle innovation and competition.

Future of AI in Legal Implications

Emerging AI Technologies and Legal Implications

As AI technology continues to evolve, new legal implications arise. Emerging AI technologies, such as autonomous vehicles, advanced robotics, and AI in healthcare, will challenge existing legal frameworks. These technologies will require careful consideration of liability, safety, and regulatory compliance.

The development of AI that can interact with the legal system itself, such as AI judges or legal advisors, will also have profound legal implications. These technologies could transform the practice of law and the administration of justice, necessitating new regulations and ethical guidelines.

Legal Considerations in AI Legal Implications

Legal considerations in the context of AI include the need for clear liability frameworks to determine who is responsible when AI causes harm. There is also a need for international cooperation to harmonize AI regulations across borders, given the global nature of AI technology and data flows.

Additionally, there is a growing call for ethical AI frameworks that guide the development and use of AI in a way that respects human rights and societal values. These frameworks would inform legal regulations and help ensure that AI benefits society as a whole.

AI in Legal Implications: Opportunities and Challenges

AI presents both opportunities and challenges in the legal realm. On the one hand, AI can improve legal processes, increase access to justice, and enhance regulatory compliance. On the other hand, it poses challenges related to accountability, transparency, and the protection of individual rights.

The legal profession must adapt to the rise of AI, with lawyers needing to understand AI technology and its implications. Lawmakers and regulators must also keep pace with AI advancements to ensure that laws remain relevant and effective in the digital age.

In conclusion, AI's legal implications are vast and complex, requiring ongoing dialogue between technologists, legal experts, policymakers, and society to navigate the challenges and harness the opportunities AI offers.

Review Questions

1. Which of the following is NOT a legal implication of AI in business?

2. What could be a legal issue in AI and Intellectual Property Rights?

3. Why are Data Protection Laws important in AI?

4. What could be a legal issue in AI and Employment Laws?

5. What is a potential legal issue in AI and Competition Laws?
6. What are some legal issues related to AI and Intellectual Property Rights?
7. How does AI intersect with Data Protection Laws?
8. What are some potential future legal implications of emerging AI technologies?

CHAPTER 17

AI and Future Business Trends

The marketing landscape is rapidly evolvin with the advent of AI technologies. AI is transforming how businesses understand and interact with their customers. Future marketing trends are likely to be dominated by AI-driven personalization, where content and product recommendations are tailored to individual consumer preferences. Predictive analytics, powered by AI, will enable marketers to anticipate customer needs and design campaigns that resonate with target audiences before they even express interest. Moreover, AI is set to revolutionize customer engagement through intelligent automation, chatbots, and virtual assistants, providing real-time, personalized interactions at scale.

Benefits of AI in Future Marketing Trends

The benefits of AI in marketing are multifaceted. AI can process vast amounts of data to glean insights that would be impossible for humans to detect, leading to more effective and targeted marketing strategies. It also allows for dynamic pricing models, where prices can be adjusted in real-time based on market demand, competition, and consumer behavior. Additionally, AI can automate repetitive tasks, freeing up human marketers to focus on creative and strategic initiatives. The use of AI in marketing also leads to improved customer experiences, as AI can quickly adapt to changing consumer preferences and provide personalized interactions.

Case Studies of AI and Future Marketing Trends

One notable case study is the use of AI by a leading e-commerce platform to personalize shopping experiences. The platform uses machine learning algorithms to analyze customer data and predict purchasing behavior, resulting in tailored product recommendations. Another example is a multinational beverage company that leverages AI to optimize its digital advertising campaigns, leading to increased engagement and higher conversion rates. These case studies demonstrate the power of AI in transforming marketing strategies and enhancing customer engagement.

AI and Future Customer Service Trends

Understanding AI and Future Customer Service Trends

AI is set to redefine customer service by providing seamless, efficient, and personalized support. Future trends indicate a shift towards AI-powered virtual agents capable of handling a wide range of customer inquiries without human intervention. These AI systems will be able to learn from each interaction, continuously improving their ability to resolve issues.

Additionally, AI will enable proactive customer service, where potential issues are identified and addressed before the customer is even aware of them. This anticipatory approach will lead to higher customer satisfaction and loyalty.

Benefits of AI in Future Customer Service Trends

The integration of AI into customer service brings numerous benefits, including 24/7 availability, instant response times, and the ability to handle large volumes of requests simultaneously. AI can also provide personalized support by accessing customer history and preferences, leading to more effective problem-solving. Furthermore, AI can identify patterns in customer inquiries, helping businesses to proactively address systemic issues and improve their products and services.

Case Studies of AI and Future Customer Service Trends

A leading telecommunications company implemented an AI chatbot to handle customer queries, resulting in a significant reduction in response times and an increase in customer satisfaction scores. Another case study involves a financial services firm that uses AI to monitor transactions in real-time, providing immediate support to customers in the event of suspected fraud. These examples highlight the transformative impact of AI on customer service operations.

AI and Future Financial Management Trends

Understanding AI and Future

Financial Management Trends

Financial management is undergoing a revolution with the integration of AI. Future trends point towards the use of AI for more accurate and timely financial analysis, enabling businesses to make data-driven decisions. AI algorithms will be able to predict market trends, assess risks, and provide insights into investment opportunities. Additionally, AI will play a crucial role in automating financial processes such as invoicing, payroll, and compliance reporting, leading to increased efficiency and reduced errors.

Benefits of AI in Future Financial Management Trends

AI offers significant benefits in financial management, including the ability to process and analyze large datasets quickly and accurately. This leads to better financial forecasting and strategic planning. AI can also detect anomalies and potential fraud, enhancing the security of financial transactions. Moreover, the automation of routine financial tasks reduces operational costs and allows finance professionals to focus on strategic activities.

Case Studies of AI and Future Financial Management Trends

A case study in the banking sector demonstrates how AI is used to personalize financial advice for customers, resulting in higher engagement and customer retention. Another example is an insurance company that employs AI to streamline claims processing, significantly reducing the time and cost associated with handling claims. These case studies illustrate the potential of AI to transform financial management practices.

AI and Future Operations and Logistics Trends

Understanding AI and Future Operations and Logistics Trends

Operations and logistics are critical areas where AI is expected to drive significant advancements. Future trends include the use of AI for optimizing supply chain management, where predictive analytics can forecast demand and automate inventory replenishment. AI will also enhance transportation logistics through route optimization and predictive maintenance of vehicles. In warehouse management, AI-powered robots and drones will streamline picking and packing processes, improving efficiency and reducing human error.

Benefits of AI in Future Operations and Logistics Trends

The benefits of AI in operations and logistics are vast, including increased efficiency, reduced costs, and improved accuracy in forecasting and inventory management. AI enables real-time decision-making, allowing businesses to respond quickly to changes in demand or supply chain disruptions. Additionally, AI can improve safety in logistics operations by predicting and preventing accidents.

Case Studies of AI and Future Operations and Logistics Trends

A leading online retailer uses AI to optimize its vast logistics network, resulting in faster delivery times and lower operational costs. Another case study involves a manufacturing company that implemented AI-driven predictive maintenance on its machinery, significantly reducing downtime and maintenance costs. These examples showcase the transformative potential of AI in operations and logistics.

Quick Facts & Statistics

AI in Operations and Logistics:

AI in Business:

AI and Future Human Resources Trends

Understanding AI and Future Human Resources Trends

AI is poised to transform human resources (HR) by automating administrative tasks and providing insights into employee performance and engagement. Future HR trends include the use of AI for talent acquisition, where algorithms can screen resumes and predict candidate success. AI will also facilitate personalized employee development programs and enhance employee engagement through data-driven insights. Furthermore, AI can assist in diversity and inclusion efforts by identifying and mitigating unconscious bias in hiring and promotion decisions.

Benefits of AI in Future Human Resources Trends

The integration of AI into HR brings numerous benefits, such as improved efficiency in recruitment processes, enhanced employee retention through predictive analytics, and more objective decision-making. AI can also help HR professionals to identify skill gaps within the organization and recommend targeted training programs. Additionally, AI-driven analytics can provide valuable insights into workforce trends, enabling better workforce planning and management.

Case Studies of AI and Future Human Resources Trends

A global technology company uses AI to enhance its recruitment process, resulting in a more diverse workforce and reduced time-to-hire. Another example is a healthcare provider that leverages AI to monitor employee well-being and reduce burnout by identifying stress patterns and suggesting interventions. These case studies highlight the positive impact of AI on HR practices.

Famous Quotes

"The future of business is in AI." - Bill Gates, Co-founder of Microsoft

"AI will be the ultimate version of Google." - Larry Page, Co-founder of Google

These quotes highlight the importance and potential impact of AI in the business world, particularly in the field of Human Resources. As AI continues to evolve, it will undoubtedly play an increasingly significant role in shaping future business trends.

AI and Future Business

Trends: A Look Ahead

Emerging AI Technologies and Future Business Trends

As AI technology continues to advance, new trends are emerging that will shape the future of business. Quantum computing, for instance, is set to exponentially increase the processing power available for AI algorithms, unlocking new possibilities in data analysis and problem-solving. Generative AI, which can create new content and designs, will empower businesses to innovate at an unprecedented pace. Additionally, the convergence of AI with other technologies like the Internet of Things (IoT) and blockchain will lead to smarter, more secure, and interconnected business ecosystems.

Challenges and Opportunities in AI and Future Business Trends

While AI presents numerous opportunities for businesses, it also poses challenges that need to be addressed. Ethical considerations, such as privacy concerns and the potential for bias in AI algorithms, are at the forefront of the discussion. There is also the challenge of ensuring that AI adoption does not lead to significant job displacement but rather complements human workers. Businesses must navigate these challenges while capitalizing on the opportunities AI offers for innovation, efficiency, and competitive advantage.

AI and Future Business Trends: A Vision for the Future

The future of business in an AI-driven world is one of limitless potential. AI has the power to unlock new levels of productivity, creativity, and growth. As businesses learn to harness the full capabilities of AI, they will be able to offer unprecedented value to their customers and stakeholders. The vision for the future is one where AI and human ingenuity combine to solve complex problems, create new markets, and drive progress across all sectors of the economy.

Review Questions

1. What is a potential benefit of AI in future marketing trends?

2. How might AI impact future customer service trends?

3. What is a potential challenge in AI and future business trends?

4. How might AI impact future operations and logistics trends?

5. What is a potential benefit of AI in future human resources trends?

6. What are some potential benefits of AI in future marketing trends?
7. How can AI influence future operations and logistics trends?
8. What are some emerging AI technologies that could influence future business trends?

CHAPTER 18

AI Implementation and Adoption

AI implementation refers to the process of integrating artificial intelligence technologies into existing business systems and workflows. It involves the practical application of AI tools and methodologies to enhance business operations, improve decision-making, and provide innovative solutions to complex problems. The goal of AI implementation is to leverage the capabilities of AI to gain a competitive edge, increase efficiency, and drive business growth.

Steps in AI Implementation

The steps in AI implementation typically include identifying business needs, selecting appropriate AI technologies, data preparation, model development, system integration, testing, and deployment. It begins with a clear understanding of the business objectives and the problems that AI can solve. Once the goals are set, businesses must gather and prepare data, which is crucial for training AI models. The development phase involves selecting algorithms, building models, and tuning them for optimal performance. After development, the AI system is integrated into the business environment, rigorously tested for reliability and accuracy, and finally deployed for use in real-world scenarios.

Challenges in AI Implementation

Implementing AI can present several challenges, including data quality and availability, choosing the right AI technology, securing stakeholder buy-in, and ensuring ethical use of AI. Data challenges are often the most significant, as AI systems require large volumes of high-quality data to function effectively. Additionally, businesses must navigate the complex landscape of AI technologies to find the most suitable solutions for their needs. Securing support from stakeholders is also critical, as AI implementation can involve significant changes to business processes. Lastly, ethical considerations such as bias, transparency, and accountability must be addressed to maintain trust and comply with regulations.

Did You Know?

AI is Everywhere!

Artificial Intelligence isn't just for big businesses. It's all around us, in places you might not expect!

So, while AI might seem like a complex and distant technology, it's actually a part of our everyday lives!

Understanding AI Adoption

What is AI Adoption?

AI adoption is the process by which businesses and individuals begin to use and integrate AI technologies into their daily operations and decision-making processes. It goes beyond implementation, focusing on the cultural and operational shifts required to fully embrace AI capabilities. Adoption involves not only the technical aspects of using AI but also the willingness of an organization's workforce to rely on and work alongside AI-driven systems.

Steps in AI Adoption

The steps in AI adoption include awareness, understanding, acceptance, integration, and optimization. Initially, businesses must become aware of AI's potential and educate their workforce about its benefits. Understanding AI's capabilities and limitations is crucial for setting realistic expectations. Acceptance involves gaining the trust of employees and stakeholders, ensuring they are comfortable with AI's role in the organization. Integration requires embedding AI into the company's culture and workflows. Finally, optimization is an ongoing process of improving AI systems and maximizing their value to the business.

Challenges in AI Adoption

Challenges in AI adoption often stem from resistance to change, lack of expertise, and concerns over job displacement. Employees may be skeptical of AI and its implications for their roles within the company. A shortage of AI talent can also hinder adoption, as businesses struggle to recruit and retain individuals with the necessary skills. Additionally, there may be fears that AI will automate jobs, leading to uncertainty and resistance. Overcoming these challenges requires clear communication, education, and reassurances about the positive impact of AI on the workforce and business outcomes.

Test Your Knowledge

Let's see how well you understood the challenges in AI adoption. Can you answer these questions?

Review the section again if you're unsure about any of the answers. Remember, understanding these challenges is key to successfully leveraging AI in business.

AI Implementation and Adoption Strategies

Developing an AI Implementation Strategy

Developing an AI implementation strategy involves setting clear objectives, assessing the technological landscape, and planning for integration. Businesses must define what they aim to achieve with AI, whether it's improving customer service, enhancing product offerings, or streamlining operations. A thorough assessment of available AI technologies and their alignment with business goals is essential. The strategy should also include a roadmap for integrating AI into existing systems, with milestones for progress and mechanisms for measuring success.

Developing an AI Adoption Strategy

An AI adoption strategy focuses on creating a culture that embraces AI. This involves training employees, fostering collaboration between human and AI systems, and establishing governance frameworks to guide ethical AI use. It's important to communicate the benefits of AI to all levels of the organization and to involve employees in the adoption process. Providing opportunities for staff to upskill and engage with AI technologies can facilitate a smoother transition and encourage a positive attitude towards AI adoption.

Case Studies of Successful AI Implementation and Adoption Strategies

Case studies of successful AI implementation and adoption often highlight the importance of leadership, clear vision, and employee engagement. For example, a retail company may implement AI for personalized product recommendations, leading to increased sales and customer satisfaction. A healthcare provider might adopt AI for predictive analytics, improving patient outcomes and operational efficiency. These case studies demonstrate how a well-executed strategy can lead to tangible benefits and serve as a blueprint for other organizations embarking on their AI journey.

AI Implementation and Adoption in Different Business Areas

AI Implementation and Adoption in Marketing

In marketing, AI implementation and adoption can revolutionize how businesses engage with customers. AI-driven analytics can provide deep insights into consumer behavior, enabling personalized marketing campaigns and content. AI tools such as chatbots can enhance customer interactions, providing immediate responses and support. By adopting AI, marketing teams can optimize their strategies, targeting the right audience at the right time with the right message, leading to improved ROI.

AI Implementation and Adoption in Customer Service

Customer service can be transformed through AI by implementing chatbots and virtual assistants to handle routine inquiries, freeing up human agents to tackle more complex issues. AI can also analyze customer interactions to identify trends and improve service quality. Adoption in this area leads to faster response times, increased customer satisfaction, and more efficient service operations.

AI Implementation and Adoption in Operations and Logistics

Operations and logistics benefit from AI through improved supply chain management, predictive maintenance, and optimized inventory levels. AI systems can forecast demand, identify potential disruptions, and suggest corrective actions. Adoption of AI in this sector leads to reduced costs, minimized downtime, and enhanced operational efficiency.

AI Implementation and Adoption in Human Resources

In human resources, AI can streamline recruitment by automating resume screening and candidate matching. AI can also assist in employee development, identifying skill gaps and recommending personalized training programs. Adoption of AI in HR enhances the employee experience, improves talent acquisition, and supports a more strategic approach to workforce management.

Future of AI Implementation

and Adoption

Emerging AI Technologies and their Impact on Implementation and Adoption

Emerging AI technologies such as quantum computing, generative AI, and advanced natural language processing are set to further revolutionize implementation and adoption. These technologies will enable more complex problem-solving, create new forms of content, and facilitate more natural interactions with AI systems. Their impact will be felt across all business areas, driving innovation and creating new opportunities for growth.

Challenges and Opportunities in AI Implementation and Adoption

The future presents both challenges and opportunities for AI implementation and adoption. Challenges include ensuring AI systems are ethical, transparent, and free from bias. There is also the need to continuously update skills and knowledge as AI technologies evolve. However, the opportunities are vast, with AI offering the potential to unlock new levels of productivity, create more personalized customer experiences, and solve previously intractable problems.

AI Implementation and Adoption: A Vision for the Future

The vision for the future of AI implementation and adoption is one of seamless integration and collaboration between humans and AI. As AI becomes more pervasive, businesses that successfully implement and adopt AI will be well-positioned to lead their industries. The future will likely see

AI as a fundamental component of business strategy, driving innovation and shaping the competitive landscape.

Review Questions

1. What does AI Implementation refer to?
2. What is a major challenge in AI Adoption?
3. What is a key step in developing an AI Implementation Strategy?
4. Which business area has seen significant impact from AI Implementation and Adoption?
5. What is a future challenge in AI Implementation and Adoption?

CHAPTER 19

AI Case Studies and Success Stories

AI in Marketing: Case Studies

Case Study 1: Ai In Digital Marketing

In the realm of digital marketing, AI has revolutionized the way companies target and engage with customers. One notable example is the use of AI by a leading e-commerce platform to personalize shopping experiences. The platform utilizes machine learning algorithms to analyze customer data, including past purchases, search history, and browsing behavior. This data is then used to create personalized product recommendations, which are displayed to customers across various digital channels. The result has been a significant increase in conversion rates and customer satisfaction, as shoppers are presented with items that closely match their interests and needs.

Another aspect of this success story is the use of AI-powered chatbots that provide instant customer support. These chatbots are capable of handling a wide range of queries, from tracking orders to product recommendations, without human intervention. By leveraging natural language processing, the chatbots can understand and respond to customer inquiries in a conversational manner, enhancing the overall user experience.

Case Study 2: AI in Content Marketing

Content marketing has been transformed by AI's ability to generate and curate content. A marketing agency specializing in content creation for clients in various industries has employed AI to streamline its content production process. The AI tool they use is capable of analyzing trending topics, keyword popularity, and competitor content to suggest content strategies that are likely to resonate with target audiences. This has allowed the agency to produce high-quality, relevant content at scale, leading to increased traffic and engagement for their clients' websites.

Moreover, the agency has implemented AI-driven analytics to monitor the performance of the content. This enables them to make data-informed decisions about which types of content are most effective, and to refine their content marketing strategies accordingly. The use of AI has not only improved efficiency but also the effectiveness of the content produced, resulting in a competitive edge for the agency and its clients.

Case Study 3: AI in Social Media Marketing

Social media marketing is another area where AI has made a significant impact. A fashion retailer leveraged AI to optimize its social media advertising campaigns. By using AI algorithms to analyze social media engagement data, the retailer was able to identify the most influential brand ambassadors and the content that generated the most engagement. This information was used to tailor social media ads to target specific demographics, leading to a higher return on investment for their advertising spend.

The retailer also used sentiment analysis, powered by AI, to gauge public perception of their brand on social media. This real-time feedback allowed them to quickly adjust their marketing strategies and address any negative sentiment, thereby maintaining a positive brand image and fostering customer loyalty.

AI in Customer Service: Case Studies

Case Study 1: AI in Customer Support

A telecommunications company implemented AI chatbots to handle customer support inquiries, resulting in a drastic reduction in response times and an increase in customer satisfaction. The chatbots were integrated into the company's website and mobile app, providing 24/7 support to customers. The AI system was trained on a vast dataset of customer service interactions, enabling it to understand and resolve a wide array of issues, from billing questions to technical support.

The chatbots' ability to learn from each interaction and improve over time has led to a continuous enhancement of the customer support experience. Additionally, the company has been able to reallocate human customer service representatives to more complex tasks, optimizing the overall efficiency of their customer service department.

Case Study 2: AI in Customer Experience

A luxury hotel chain implemented an AI-powered concierge service to enhance the guest experience. The virtual concierge is accessible via smartphones and uses AI to provide personalized recommendations for dining, entertainment, and local attractions based on the guest's preferences and past behavior. The system also allows guests to make reservations and requests directly through the AI interface, streamlining the service process.

This innovative approach to customer service has not only improved guest satisfaction but has also provided the hotel with valuable insights into guest preferences, enabling them to tailor their services and offerings more effectively. The success of the virtual concierge has set a new standard for personalized guest experiences in the hospitality industry.

Case Study 3: AI in Customer Retention

A software-as-a-service (SaaS) company utilized AI to predict customer churn and improve retention rates. By analyzing customer usage data, support ticket history, and payment patterns, the AI model identified at-risk customers who were likely to cancel their subscriptions. The company then proactively reached out to these customers with personalized offers and support, successfully reducing churn.

The AI system also provided insights into the common factors contributing to customer dissatisfaction, allowing the company to address underlying issues and improve their product and services. As a result, the company not only retained valuable customers but also enhanced its reputation for excellent customer service.

Quick Facts & Statistics

AI in Customer Service

AI in Customer Retention

AI in Business

AI in Financial Management: Case Studies

Case Study 1: AI in Financial Analysis

A multinational corporation implemented AI to automate its financial analysis and reporting processes. The AI system was designed to extract data from various financial documents, consolidate the information, and generate comprehensive reports. This automation reduced the time required for financial analysis from weeks to days, allowing the finance team to focus on strategic decision-making rather than data processing.

The AI system also employed predictive analytics to forecast future financial trends based on historical data, enabling the company to make more informed investment decisions and better manage its financial resources. The accuracy and efficiency of the AI-driven financial analysis have given the corporation a competitive edge in financial planning and management.

Case Study 2: AI in Risk Management

A leading bank integrated AI into its risk management framework to identify and mitigate potential risks. The AI model was trained on a large dataset of financial transactions to detect patterns indicative of fraudulent activity. By implementing real-time monitoring of transactions, the bank was able to flag and investigate suspicious activity much more quickly than with traditional methods.

The AI-driven risk management system not only enhanced the bank's ability to prevent fraud but also reduced the number of false positives, minimizing the inconvenience to customers. This proactive approach to risk management has bolstered the bank's reputation for security and reliability.

Case Study 3: AI in Investment Strategies

An investment firm employed AI to optimize its investment strategies. The AI algorithms analyzed vast amounts of financial data, including market trends, economic indicators, and company performance, to identify the most promising investment opportunities. The firm's portfolio managers used these insights to make data-driven investment decisions, resulting in higher returns for their clients.

The AI system also provided scenario analysis, allowing the firm to assess the potential impact of various market events on their investments. This level of analysis was instrumental in developing robust investment strategies that could withstand market volatility. The success of the AI-driven investment approach has attracted significant attention in the financial industry, showcasing the potential of AI in asset management.

AI in Operations and Logistics: Case Studies

Case Study 1: AI in Supply Chain Management

A global manufacturing company implemented AI to enhance its supply chain management. The AI system provided real-time visibility into the supply chain, predicting potential disruptions and suggesting alternative routes and suppliers to mitigate risks. This proactive approach allowed the company to maintain a steady flow of materials and products, even in the face of unforeseen events such as natural disasters or supplier bankruptcies.

The AI-driven supply chain management also enabled the company to optimize inventory levels, reducing waste and storage costs. The efficiency gains from the AI implementation have had a significant impact on the company's bottom line and its ability to deliver products to customers on time.

Case Study 2: AI in Inventory Management

A retail chain utilized AI to revolutionize its inventory management. The AI system analyzed sales data, seasonal trends, and consumer behavior to predict future demand for products. This predictive capability allowed the retailer to stock the right products in the right quantities, minimizing overstock and stockouts.

The AI-driven inventory management system also identified opportunities for cost savings by optimizing the timing and quantity of reorders. The retailer experienced a marked improvement in inventory turnover and a reduction in lost sales due to out-of-stock situations, demonstrating the power of AI in retail operations.

Case Study 3: AI in Delivery and Distribution

A logistics company integrated AI into its delivery and distribution operations to improve efficiency and customer satisfaction. The AI system optimized delivery routes in real-time, taking into account traffic conditions, delivery windows, and vehicle capacity. This optimization led to a reduction in delivery times and fuel consumption, resulting in cost savings and a lower environmental impact.

The company also used AI to predict delivery delays and communicate proactively with customers, enhancing transparency and trust. The success of the AI implementation in delivery and distribution has set a new industry standard for logistics operations.

Further Reading

If you're interested in learning more about how AI is revolutionizing the logistics and delivery industry, here are some recommended resources:

These resources will give you a deeper understanding of the practical applications of AI in logistics and delivery, and the potential benefits and challenges of AI implementation in this industry.

AI in Human Resources: Case Studies

Case Study 1: AI in Recruitment

A technology firm leveraged AI to transform its recruitment process. The AI system screened resumes and applications to identify the most suitable candidates for open positions, significantly reducing the time and effort required for initial candidate evaluations. The AI tool also helped to eliminate unconscious bias by focusing on skills and experience rather than demographic factors.

The firm's recruiters used the insights provided by the AI system to conduct more targeted interviews, leading to a higher quality of hires. The AI-driven recruitment process has not only improved the efficiency of the hiring process but also contributed to a more diverse and talented workforce.

Case Study 2: AI in Employee Engagement

A multinational corporation implemented an AI-powered platform to enhance employee engagement. The platform analyzed employee feedback and engagement survey data to identify areas of concern and opportunities for improvement. By leveraging AI, the company was able to take a data-driven approach to employee engagement, implementing targeted initiatives that led to an increase in employee satisfaction and retention.

The AI system also provided personalized recommendations for employee development, helping individuals to grow their skills and advance their careers within the company. The positive impact on employee morale and productivity has been a testament to the effectiveness of AI in human resources management.

Case Study 3: AI in Performance Management

A financial services firm used AI to modernize its performance management system. The AI tool analyzed performance data to provide employees with real-time feedback and actionable insights into their work. This ongoing feedback loop allowed employees to continuously improve their performance and align their efforts with the company's strategic goals.

The AI-driven performance management system also helped managers to identify high performers and potential leaders within the organization, facilitating more effective succession planning. The firm's investment in AI for performance management has resulted in a more motivated and high-performing workforce.

AI Success Stories: A Look at the Future

Success Story 1: AI in Emerging Businesses

An emerging fintech startup utilized AI to disrupt the traditional banking industry. The startup developed an AI-powered personal finance assistant that provides users with personalized financial advice and automated money management. The assistant uses machine learning to analyze users' financial transactions and habits, offering tailored recommendations for saving, investing, and budgeting.

The success of the AI personal finance assistant has attracted a large user base and significant venture capital investment, positioning the startup as a leader in the fintech space. The company's innovative use of AI has demonstrated the potential for emerging businesses to leverage AI to create new market opportunities and challenge established players.

Success Story 2: AI in Established Businesses

A well-established automotive manufacturer integrated AI across its operations to maintain its competitive edge. The manufacturer used AI to optimize its manufacturing processes, reducing production times and improving quality control. AI algorithms also enabled the company to design more efficient and safer vehicles by simulating and analyzing various design scenarios.

The manufacturer's commitment to AI has not only enhanced its operational efficiency but also led to the development of innovative products, such as autonomous vehicles. The company's success story illustrates how established businesses can use AI to innovate and stay ahead in a rapidly evolving market.

Success Story 3: AI in Innovative Business Models

A health tech company developed an AI-powered platform that revolutionized patient care. The platform uses AI to analyze medical data, including electronic health records, imaging, and genetic information, to assist doctors in diagnosing and treating diseases. The AI system can identify patterns and correlations that may be missed by human analysis, leading to more accurate diagnoses and personalized treatment plans.

The health tech company's AI platform has improved patient outcomes and reduced healthcare costs, showcasing the transformative potential of AI in creating innovative business models that address critical societal needs.

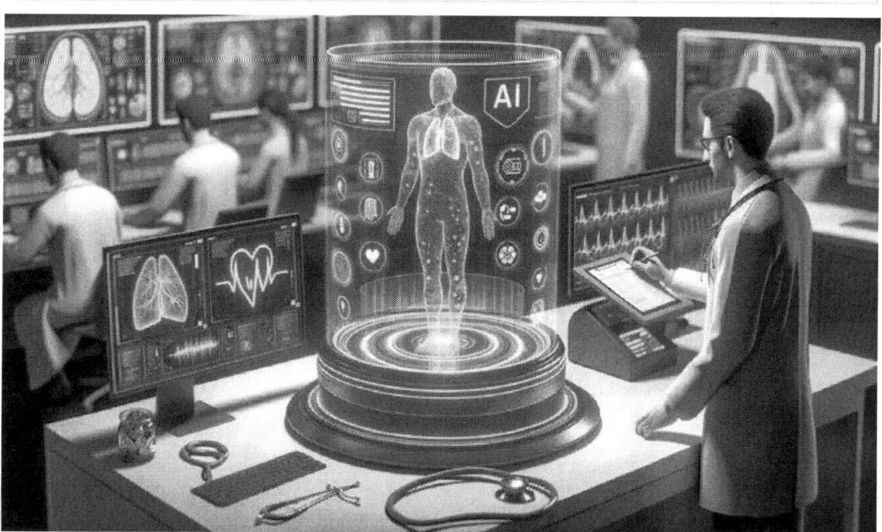

These case studies and success stories provide a glimpse into the diverse applications of AI across various industries and the profound impact it can have on business operations, customer engagement, and market competitiveness. As AI technology continues to advance, it is clear that its role in shaping the future of business is only set to increase, offering exciting opportunities for innovation and growth.

Review Questions

1. Which of the following is NOT a way AI has been used in marketing, according to the case studies?
2. In the context of AI in Customer Service, what was the focus of Case Study 3?
3. Which case study focused on the use of AI in Risk Management?
4. What was the focus of the third case study in the AI in Operations and Logistics section?
5. Which of the following is NOT a focus of the AI Success Stories presented in the chapter?

CHAPTER 20

Conclusion and Next Steps

Key Takeaways from the Book

Throughout this book, we have explored the multifaceted role of artificial intelligence (AI) in the business world. We have learned that AI is not just a technological advancement but a transformative force that is reshaping industries, creating new opportunities, and posing unique challenges. Key takeaways include the understanding that AI can optimize operations, enhance customer experiences, and provide invaluable insights through data analysis. We have also seen that while AI can be a powerful tool for growth, it requires careful consideration of ethical implications and strategic planning for successful integration.

Importance of AI in Business

AI's importance in business cannot be overstated. It has become a critical component for maintaining competitive advantage, driving innovation, and achieving operational excellence. AI technologies help businesses to automate routine tasks, make better decisions, and personalize customer interactions. As we have seen, companies that leverage AI effectively can expect to see significant improvements in efficiency, productivity, and profitability.

Future of AI in Business

The future of AI in business is bright and full of potential. As AI technologies continue to evolve, they will become more accessible and integrated into every aspect of business operations. We can anticipate further advancements in machine learning, natural language processing, and robotics, all of which will open new avenues for innovation. The businesses that stay ahead of the curve by adopting and adapting to these technologies will be well-positioned to thrive in the ever-changing business landscape.

Next Steps in AI Learning

Resources for Further Learning

To continue your journey in AI learning, a wealth of resources is available. Online platforms such as Coursera, edX, and Udacity offer courses ranging from introductory to advanced levels. Books, academic journals, and research papers provide in-depth knowledge on specific AI topics. Additionally, attending AI conferences and webinars can keep you updated on the latest trends and research findings. Visit www.christopherdessi.com to sign up for my newsletter and to stay informed.

Courses and Certifications in AI

For those seeking structured learning, numerous courses and certifications are available. These programs cover various aspects of AI, including algorithms, data science, and ethical considerations. Certifications from recognized institutions can add value to your professional profile and demonstrate your commitment to understanding and applying AI in business contexts. Visit www.christopherdessi.com for courses and more.

Communities and Forums for AI Enthusiasts

Engaging with communities and forums is an excellent way to connect with other AI enthusiasts. Platforms like GitHub, Stack Overflow, and Reddit host vibrant communities where individuals can share knowledge, collaborate on projects, and seek advice. Local meetups and special interest groups also provide opportunities for networking and learning from peers.

Quick Facts & Statistics

Artificial Intelligence in Business:

AI Communities:

Next Steps in AI Implementation

Developing an AI Strategy for Your Business

Developing an AI strategy is crucial for ensuring that AI implementation aligns with your business goals. This strategy should encompass identifying business areas that can benefit from AI, setting clear objectives, and establishing metrics for success. It should also consider the ethical implications of AI deployment and include plans for managing data privacy and security.

Finding the Right AI Tools and Technologies

With a plethora of AI tools and technologies available, selecting the right ones for your business can be daunting. It is essential to assess the compatibility of these tools with your existing systems, their scalability, and the level of support provided. Open-source tools can be a cost-effective option, while proprietary solutions may offer more specialized features and dedicated support.

Building an AI Team

A skilled AI team is the backbone of successful AI implementation. This team should consist of data scientists, AI engineers, and domain experts who can work together to develop and deploy AI solutions. Investing in training and development for your team will ensure they remain up-to-date with the latest AI advancements and best practices.

Did You Know?

Artificial Intelligence is not just about creating robots or science-fiction. It's a significant part of our everyday lives and is used in a variety of sectors, including business.

AI in Everyday Life

AI in Business

Businesses use AI in various ways to increase efficiency and profitability. Here are a few examples:

Next Steps in AI Adoption

Promoting AI Adoption in Your Organization

Promoting AI adoption requires a top-down approach, with leadership setting the tone for a culture that embraces innovation. Educating employees about the benefits of AI and involving them in the adoption process can help alleviate fears and resistance. Demonstrating quick wins and sharing success stories can also build momentum and support for AI initiatives.

Overcoming Challenges in AI Adoption

Challenges in AI adoption can range from technical hurdles to organizational resistance. Addressing these challenges involves ensuring that your technology infrastructure can support AI applications, providing adequate training for employees, and establishing clear communication channels to address concerns and feedback. It is also important to manage expectations and be prepared for a gradual adoption process.

Case Studies of Successful AI Adoption

Learning from case studies of successful AI adoption can provide valuable insights. These case studies often highlight best practices, common pitfalls to avoid, and innovative approaches to problem-solving. By studying how other businesses have navigated the AI adoption journey, you can apply these lessons to your own organization's efforts.

Looking Ahead: The Future of AI and Business

Emerging AI Technologies and Their Potential Impact

Emerging AI technologies such as quantum computing, generative adversarial networks, and reinforcement learning are set to have a profound impact on business. These technologies promise to unlock new capabilities in processing power, content creation, and autonomous decision-making, potentially revolutionizing how businesses operate and compete.

AI and the Future of Different Business Areas

AI is expected to continue its integration into various business areas, including marketing, customer service, operations, and human resources. In marketing, AI will enable more personalized and targeted campaigns. In customer service, AI chatbots and virtual assistants will provide more efficient and satisfying customer interactions. Operations will see increased automation and predictive maintenance, while human resources will benefit from AI-driven recruitment and talent management.

AI and the Future of Business: A Vision for the Future

The future of business with AI is one of collaboration between humans and machines, where AI augments human capabilities and enables more informed decision-making. As AI becomes more pervasive, businesses that can adapt and innovate will be better positioned to meet the needs of their customers and stay ahead of the competition. The vision for the future is one where AI not only drives profitability but also contributes to a more sustainable and equitable world.

Review Questions

1. What is a key takeaway from the book?
2. What is a recommended next step in AI learning?
3. What is a crucial step in AI implementation?
4. What is a key factor in promoting AI adoption in your organization?
5. What is a potential impact of emerging AI technologies on business?
6. What are some resources for further learning in AI?
7. What are some key steps in developing an AI strategy

for your business?

8. What are some potential impacts of emerging AI technologies on business?

FOR ADDITIONAL RESOURCES ON HOW TO PROFIT WITH AI:

www.christopherdessi.com/resources

ABOUT THE AUTHOR

Christopher Dessi

Chris Dessi stands at the forefront of technological innovation, embodying the rare ability to "skate to where the puck is going" in the rapidly evolving digital landscape. As the visionary Chief Revenue Officer at Diamond Standard Co., Chris spearheads the strategic growth, technological advancement, and market expansion of the world's inaugural regulated diamond commodity. His role is pivotal in revolutionizing the diamond supply chain, introducing unprecedented transparency and efficiency, and empowering investors with a transformative hard asset that seamlessly integrates with blockchain technology.

With a dynamic career spanning over two decades in the technology sector, Chris has cemented his reputation as a trailblazer in sales and marketing. His strategic acumen and entrepreneurial spirit have been instrumental in scaling and steering software companies like Buddy Media and Silverback Social to remarkable successes. Chris's passion for innovation extends beyond corporate achievements; he is deeply committed to generating value for investors, customers, and partners alike, while fostering a culture of empowerment and mentorship within his teams.

An acclaimed author, Chris has penned three best-selling books that delve into the intersections of technology, business, and personal development. His insights have graced the stage of a TEDx talk, earning him numerous accolades for leadership and innovation. A certified Scrum Master, Chris's expertise is recognized across the industry, with features in prestigious publications such as Forbes, Fortune, Success, and Sports Illustrated. His compelling keynote presentations have captivated audiences from the United States Marines to leading technology conferences worldwide.

At the heart of Chris's drive is a mission to democratize the diamond market, making it accessible and navigable for investors through cutting-edge blockchain tokens. His work not only signifies a leap towards the future of finance but also exemplifies his knack for anticipating and shaping the trajectory of new technology. Chris Dessi is not just part of the technological revolution; he is leading it, ensuring that both his team and his innovations are always a step ahead in the game.

Made in the USA
Columbia, SC
29 April 2024

17fd692a-a6b3-4f1a-9a66-ce6b2cc752d9R01